For The Love Of Naomi

LORRAINE WYLIE

AMBASSADOR INTERNATIONAL
Greenville, South Carolina • Belfast, Northern Ireland

THE LOVE OF NAOMI
© Copyright 2007 Lorraine Wylie

ISBN 978-1-84030-191-5

Ambassador Publications
a division of
Ambassador Productions Ltd.
Providence House
Ardenlee Street,
Belfast,
BT6 8QJ
Northern Ireland
www.ambassador-productions.com

Emerald House
427 Wade Hampton Blvd.
Greenville
SC 29609, USA
www.emeraldhouse.com

AUTHOR'S DEDICATION

As with my previous books I would like to dedicate 'For The Love Of Naomi' to my husband, Michael, my children, Christopher, Jonathan and Kathryn and not forgetting, Jane, my daughter-in-law. I have always found the love, support and encouragement of my family an invaluable source of inspiration.

Lorraine Wylie

ABOUT THE AUTHOR

Lorraine contributes to a variety of Christian and secular publications and writes regularly for Lifetimes magazine. She lives on a smallholding in south-west France with her husband, Michael, who is an artist. The couple have three children, a daughter-in-law, two cats, six chickens and a rooster.

Lorraine's previous titles include 'Iris, An Intimate Portrait,' 'What Do You Mean It's Impossible!' and 'Is There Another One?'

Contents

AUTHOR'S NOTE

Although all the events recorded in this book are true I considered it appropriate, for reasons of discretion and to avoid un-necessary embarrassment to anyone, to alter the names of certain people and places.

Lorraine Wylie
September 2007

E-mail : lorrainewylie@orange.fr

Billy, Mary and Naomi

Naomi

The Stevenson Family

Prologue
A CHILD IS BORN
ॐ

It was a difficult and protracted labour but delivery did not bring tears of relief. At the sight of her baby daughter the woman turned her face to the wall and wept. She knew that this child would not be greeted with welcoming smiles or good wishes for health and prosperity. In a poverty stricken culture where gender determined the difference between life and death, the little girl had no future. Male relatives greeted news of the child's arrival with a shake of the head, her existence of little consequence. Impotent to help, sympathy filled the women's eyes in a silent expression of female camaraderie

Barely recovered from the exhaustion of birth, the young mother rose and looked at her tiny daughter. The umbilical cord that had provided pre-natal sustenance remained uncut but circumstances had already severed any hope of continued maternal nurture. Circumscribed by culture as well as gender she was powerless to alter her baby's destiny. Wrapping the infant against the chill of a South Korean winter, she carefully pinned a piece of paper to the threadbare cloth. Motherhood had not afforded her the right to decide the child's future or the power to prevent her death yet, by giving her child a name, the Korean mother, not only acknowledged the little girl's existence, she gave the only gift at her disposal. In monetary terms it was a bequest of little value but, in the currency of human dignity, a name conveys identity which, in any culture, is a priceless asset.

Perhaps in a year or so she would nurse another baby. A son and heir would comfort and soothe the ache that now filled her empty arms and heart. No doubt, in quiet moments the young mother would remember the child for whom a city pavement made a cold crib. Although snatched from her life, the daughter she had named Kyung Sook Kim, would live in her heart.

Cocooned and protected by infantile dreams, the tiny form knew nothing of her peril. Helpless and vulnerable she lay at the mercy of the elements and the cruelty of man's indifference. But the little scrap of humanity was the object of divine mercy and compassion even before she was born. Kyung Sook Kim may have entered the world in 1975 but God's preparation for her future took place fourteen years earlier when, three weeks before Christmas, a working class couple embarked on a journey that would lead them far from their Northern Irish home and into the life of the Korean child.

Chapter 1
THE STORY BEGINS

ON THE 9th December 1961 at 11:00 am, Mary McMillan jumped from the frying pan into the fire. Instead of a father addicted to drink, her future was now linked to an alcoholic husband. As she stood on the steps of St Stephen's Church in Belfast, radiant in her fashionable ballerina length dress, rose tinted spectacles were not part of the wedding attire. The new Mrs Stevenson was under no illusions about the kind of man she had just married.

From the age of fifteen Billy Stevenson had been the source of his family's heartache as well as the subject of their prayers. His parents, Christians since their son was just nine years old, had hoped that the influence of Sunday school, children's meetings and regular gospel missions would lead Billy toward salvation. But as adolescence awakened the passions of youth, it was drinking dens and not gospel halls that whetted the teenage appetite. His first job at Mackey's Foundry in Belfast had introduced him to the world of more adult pastimes. The odd game of darts was of little consequence but wagers and gambling rapidly became routine. Within a couple of years the young lad had developed not only an insatiable thirst for drink, but a constant craving for excitement and adventure. At every opportunity the seventeen year old rebelled against parental counsel, refusing to heed either pleas or warnings. Eventually, in a bid to escape the sheltered confines of his Christian home, Billy attempted to join the Navy but when that failed, he lied about his age, offered his services to both Queen and country and joined the army instead. His parents were broken hearted but they knew their son's determined character and so, resigned to the situation, they accompanied him to the dock where, after a tearful farewell, they waved goodbye and committed him to God.

It didn't take long for Corporal William Stevenson of the Royal Inniskilling Fusiliers to discover that discipline rather than adventure was the definition of military life. Dreams of travel and exotic destinations were totally eclipsed by the mundane reality of a German barracks where shining boots and scrubbing floors proved a poor substitute for the thrill of daring escapades. Taking orders also posed a problem for the lad who, since childhood, had resisted the restrictive reins of authority. Even his move to the Royal Engineers, a decision influenced greatly by Billy's friend, Jonny McQuade, who had served in the famous Chindits, didn't bring satisfaction. However, it wasn't only regimental routine that unsettled the young soldier. Billy also suffered a huge dose of love sickness. No matter where he went, his heart remained firmly anchored in Belfast. From their first teenage encounter, Mary McMillan had remained the love of his life, although at one point, it seemed that Billy's teenage charm had captured the wrong heart. Initially it was Mary's friend who dreamed of the handsome youth and eventually sent Mary to ask for a date. But one look at the pretty messenger and Billy was smitten. From that moment the pair became inseparable. Fortunately, apart from a dented ego, Mary's chum suffered no permanent damage and her heart, as well as the friendship remained intact. With regular letters and postcards, Billy continued to woo and court his sweetheart until finally she agreed to marry him. As soon as possible, he grasped the opportunity to return to Belfast where, three weeks before Christmas, he married Mary McMillan and entered into yet another, more binding contract that demanded a lifelong allegiance of the heart.

As they left St Stephen's Church, the bride and groom may have been deliriously happy but among the guests, Mary's mother hid her anxiety with a smile. She knew the kind of life Mary had chosen. Mrs McMillan understood the effect of alcohol on both home and marriage and realised the years of worry and loneliness that waited her daughter. Billy's parents also offered their congratulations yet they too harboured concern. They had no doubt that their son loved his new wife. The problem was that he loved alcohol more. From the human point of view, the prognosis for the couple's future happiness was poor.

Regardless of what anyone said, Mary Stevenson knew that Billy had a good-natured spirit. She had seen a side to her new husband that few glimpsed. Often she had witnessed a sensitivity and gentleness that was rare among the working class men of her generation. Other husbands may claim to treat their women like queens but Mary knew the limited realms of such kingdoms. For many women, the confines of home, especially the kitchen, formed the boundaries of their influence and jurisdiction. Billy, however, had always treated her as an equal. They shared the same sense of humour and he had the knack of turning her frown into a smile. More importantly, Billy made her feel special. Growing up in a home where life was choreographed to alcohol's unpredictable tune, Mary had discovered that the easiest way to survive was to blend with her surroundings and learn to disappear. Being noticed was a novel and exciting experience! Love may have set her pulse racing and tied her stomach in knots but it had not affected the young woman's vision. It was clear that the man she loved had a real problem. By any standards, his drinking habit was excessive, although in a community where a pub culture was part of the social fabric, he was by no means unique. Her new husband may be a little rough around the edges but Mary, with the confidence of youth, believed that with daily doses of her special brand of love, Billy would soon lose any desire or need of alcohol. The responsibilities of married life would prove a happy and sobering experience. In her opinion, their marriage had all the ingredients for success.

It was during their honeymoon that reality set in and Mary began to realise she had a demanding and serious rival for her husband's affections. Without the animation of summer tourists, the promenade in the seaside town of Bangor, County Down, was windswept and empty. Yet, regardless of the season, the little town should have been an oasis for youthful dreams of love and romance. Instead, the young bride felt the chill of loneliness and watched helplessly as Billy courted the other love of his life. From the day they celebrated their marriage until the moment they returned from honeymoon, Billy Stevenson was constantly drunk. Mary's first experience of married life was a reminder of years gone by and a foretaste of those to come. Still, she refused to admit defeat. Marriage was important to her and she was determined to make it work. After all it was still early days and, as the forlorn bride repeatedly told herself, love needs time.

Six months later the honeymoon was well and truly over. Neither Billy's dislike for army life nor his desire for marital domesticity had proven sufficient grounds for military discharge. Equally, authority's failure to appreciate his situation did not seem adequate reason for him to return voluntarily to army routine. Instead, he decided that Her Majesty had sufficient numbers to offer protection and didn't need Billy Stevenson. Despite breaking his military contract, the young soldier believed that life as a civilian was more appealing and determined to remain in Belfast. But his freedom was short lived. After a noisy brawl in a local bar at Townsend Street on Belfast's Shankill Road, Billy found himself hurled through the doorway into the welcoming arms of the Military Police. Before he knew what was happening, the reluctant recruit was detained at Lisburn's Theipval Barracks before being returned to his regiment in Germany. His new wife was back to the old courtship routine of conducting their relationship by post.

Eventually, with his time served, Billy was released but his military experience had done little to sate either his appetite for adventure or his favourite glass of stout. His young wife had done her best to create a warm and loving atmosphere. She had tried to turn their first home in North Boundary Street and later at Highfield Estate into a cosy cocoon of domestic bliss. But no matter how big the dose or how often applied, love had failed to tame Billy Stevenson. In fact he was getting worse. Not only was his constant drinking causing problems, his venture into the shady world of Belfast's racketeering was also affecting their marriage. Theft from local shops made him a nuisance to the community but his worst crime was against the woman he claimed to love. He had robbed Mary Stevenson of peace as well as her right to happiness.

As he spiralled out of control, Billy's parents were also in deep despair. Reasoning, pleading and even prayer appeared to have little effect. They had taught their son the scriptures, trained him from childhood and could not understand the direction he had chosen. It wasn't that Billy didn't know the way of salvation. Every Saturday on his way to place a bet with the local bookmakers, he had to run the gambit of open air meetings. Time and again, much to his annoyance, little tracts with messages of God's love and forgiveness were pressed into his reluctant hands. No doubt, the scriptures, had been etched clearly on his mind, they just hadn't rooted in his heart. Billy simply did not want to know about either God or eternity. For him, the present and the way of the world seemed much more exciting. As he delved deeper in search of freedom and thrills, he didn't notice the bonds that tightened and bound him to a life of misery and sin.

The second birth for the Stevenson's added a beautiful baby girl to the family circle. Like her brother, little Isabelle also received a pet name. From the moment Mary set eyes on her daughter, the title of 'angel' seemed to sum up the infant's innocent charm. There was no doubt that Billy loved both of his children but paternal emotion wasn't strong enough to release him from the bonds of addiction. The arrival of a son and daughter may have changed the family dynamics, nevertheless Billy remained drunk and, during hospital visiting hours, Mary was still alone. Two subsequent pregnancies brought a full portion of misery and heartache. Despite being full term, both babies died. It appeared that Mary's rare blood group proved an insurmountable obstacle to delivering any more healthy children. Medical experts, moved with compassion and concern, counselled her against further attempts at motherhood. Bringing children into the world was, for her, a difficult event that required care and constant attention. As well as the expertise of gynaecologists and obstetricians, she needed the emotional support of a considerate and dependable husband. It would prove difficult to find a kinder man but reliability was not one of Billy's strong points. Within a relatively short space of time, Mary had experienced motherhood's indescribable joy as well as its pain.

For many women, Friday afternoon on Belfast's Shankill Road offered more than a shopper's paradise. As well as a prime cut of beef or a plump roast chicken for Sunday's dinner, housewives seized the opportunity for a slice of gossip and a cup of tea! At every street corner or in one of the many fish and chip saloons, mothers, accompanied by babies in prams and laughing children, gathered to share the latest calamity or celebration of family life. In fact, over the decades, the weekly event had adopted all the characteristics of an enjoyable tradition rather than a routine chore. While women searched for bargains or traded recipes over endless pots of strongly brewed tea, their husbands often passed the time with the simple but popular game of pitch and toss, hoping to win a few extra pennies for a bet on the Saturday horse races.

However, interspersed among the grocery stores and butcher shops, was a wide variety of public houses and drinking clubs that, as the evening wore on, proved an irresistible port of call. By mid-night most, if not all, of the weeks wages was spent on alcohol. It was a dent in the family budget that few women could afford and, in an attempt to minimise the loss, some decided to intercept their husband on the drinking route, salvaging enough money to buy groceries for the week ahead. But Mary Stevenson knew the futility of such actions. Experience had taught her that best way to handle an alcoholic man was to simply wait it out. For the young Mrs Stevenson, the weekend normally began in the early hours of Saturday morning with the sound of splintering wood and her husband's shouts of annoyance. It didn't matter how often she reminded him to take the key, Billy's arrival always meant a visit to the locksmith. On one occasion, the craftsman suggested it might be risky, but cheaper if Mary simply left the door unlocked. Short of cash and upset with Billy, she decided to take the experts advice. Instead of waiting for her husband to weave his way unsteadily home, she went to bed and left him to fend for himself. Her actions were to save his life.

Pub or gang fights were part and parcel of inner city life. Despite his problems, Billy Stevenson was not naturally aggressive. However, disagreements that ended in brawls were not uncommon and, more often than not, Billy landed, as well as received, his share of punches. His wife was used to her husband's occasional black eye but when a few heavy clouts removed his teeth, Billy and Mary were introduced to the embarrassing world of denture mishaps. They soon discovered that the pearly whites could float in beer glasses as well fly across a room at the most unlikely moments! While bruised limbs, black eyes and even false teeth may have been painful and embarrassing reminders of a drink fuelled scuffle, the young father suffered an attack that, but for the grace of God, would have cost his life. After a beating that left him lying in the gutter for hours, Billy Stevenson eventually managed to stumble home. Although, on this occasion he didn't have the strength to kick his way into the house. Wakened by the noise, Mary, despite her resolution to ignore him, came down and tried to haul her husband upstairs to bed. But his weight proved too much for her slender frame and she was unable to do more than guide him into the living room where he spent the night slumped upright in a chair. The next morning, annoyance and anger turned to fear when Mary noticed her husband's pallor and confused, erratic behaviour. Immediately, running to her neighbour's home she screamed for someone to fetch the doctor who, as soon as he saw the patient, realised the serious nature of his injury. Billy Stevenson spent the next four weeks in hospital suffering from a severely fractured skull.   Doctors later confirmed that, only the fact that he had spent the night in an upright position had saved his life.

As the violence began to spread across the Province, few families escaped the terror. Like most women, Mary worried constantly about her husband's safety. When he was late home, her imagination went into overdrive as she tortured herself with every possible scenario.   Undoubtedly, in every strata of social life, peace was the casualty. Yet, whatever drama Mary's mind managed to conjure up, she could never have envisaged the starring role she would play in one of Belfast's nightmare scenarios. Not only did it land her at the centre of a murder trial. It also brought her face to face with God.

When a local youth stopped for a chat, he had no idea that, the day was anything but ordinary. He did not know that Mary Stevenson was the last person he would see before entering eternity. Joking and laughing, the couple exchanged pleasantries unaware that the minutes of the young man's life were ticking away. Suddenly, as the sound of gunfire rent the air, Mary watched with horrified disbelief as the lad fell wounded and helpless to the ground. Normality fled as pandemonium erupted. Screaming, children ran in disorientated circles, while neighbours rushed to help drag the unconscious victim into Mary's home. Dashing upstairs in search of blankets and pillow, the terrified mother struggled to make sense of events. It seemed incredible that such violence should take place in her street, never mind on her actual doorstep. Despite the immediate arrival of police and ambulances, it was obvious that death had already claimed its prey. Shocked and devastated at the waste of a young life, the community mourned its loss. However, for Mary, the situation was from over.

When suspects were arrested and then charged, Mary, like everyone else, followed the local media reports of the trial. However, she was about to be pushed into a role she didn't want. One evening, two strangers called to her home and asked if she'd witnessed the identity of the youth's murderer. Perplexed as well as a little intimidated by the visitors' attitude, Mary truthfully admitted that she had not seen the person who carried out the crime. In the next few moments her nightmare was well and truly under way. Showing her a photograph of the youth who had been charged with the murder, the strangers informed her that, when called as a witness, she must testify that she had seen this particular man pull the trigger. Any refusal to comply would put her family's safety in jeopardy. She did not have an option.

As the weeks passed, Billy learned that his wife would be the last witness to be summoned. There was nothing anyone could do. Stress levels soared as Mary entered a tug of war between her conscience and fear for her family's life. By the time eleven weeks had elapsed, Mary was a complete bundle of nerves. The constant media attention ensured that every testimony made headline news. Even as she made her way to the court house, the terrified woman, was desperately trying to find some way out. She could not tell lies and send a possibly innocent man to prison. Neither could she bear the thought of what would happen to Billy and other members of her family if she told the truth.   Just before her court appearance she made one last attempt to appeal to the paramilitary gang. Begging them to re-consider, Mary pleaded for mercy. But with neither pity nor compassion, her blackmailers insisted she either comply or take her family and leave the country. When she turned again toward the courthouse, Mary had never felt so hopeless.   At her wit's end, the frightened woman did what we all do when we reach that point of utter helplessness. On the steps of the courthouse, she remembered the God of her youth in whom she had placed a childish trust. Many years had passed but she knew He would not let her down. There in full view of the passing public, she bowed and asked that God release her from this awful task.

As she entered the court room, the public gallery was packed to capacity and at the sight of the defendant, began to jeer and shout.   Slowly, amidst the uproar, her heart pounding, Mary made her way to the witness box, with tears trickling down her face she prepared to take the stand. Suddenly, just as she reached the step, her prayer was miraculously answered. With a mixture of relief, joy and shock, she heard the judge demand that the courtroom be cleared immediately. He had decreed that, because of the disruption, the trial should continue in closed session and the jury alone should decide the verdict. The last witness would not be required.   Mary was free to go. That was the first of many dramatic answers to prayer for Mary Stevenson. She had turned to the Lord and found Him faithful. Before long she would know the joy of having her relationship with Him fully restored.

moments playing in the building site opposite, young Billy and Isabelle Stevenson rushed into their aunt's home carrying a bag of 'treasure' they had discovered amongst the ruins. The last thing Mary's sister needed was trash all over her nice clean floor and so Mary ordered her children to take their 'treasure' outside where they could play in the street. However, a few minutes later she noticed that neighbours were rapidly surrounding her son and daughter and a sense of agitated excitement filled the air. Curious to know what was happening, she pushed her way to the front of the crowd. There amidst the dust and debris lay a pile of sparkling gold. Isabelle and William looked expectantly at their mother, unable to comprehend the sudden change in attitude. Just a few moments previously they and their 'treasure' had been thrown unceremoniously out of the house. Suddenly their mum, as well as the whole neighbourhood wanted a share! Within a few days, the Stevensons' find hit the headlines and Belfast was gripped by an intense bout of gold fever. Fortunately for Mary, she was not around when her husband learned how she'd thrown away a bag of gold sovereigns and their only chance for prosperity! But while the unexpected discovery may have provided a few luxuries, it would also have funded Billy's addiction and without doubt purchased his death. Thankfully, God had riches of a more lasting value in store for the Stevenson family.

Billy's alcoholic lifestyle continued to cause his wife and children untold misery but on one occasion, it almost led to a rendezvous with death. Fuelled by drink and completely irrational, the father of two decided to take his family for an afternoon drive. The unsafe condition of the vehicle combined with her husband's inebriated state certainly spiked Mary's terror but arrival at their destination did nothing to lower the stress levels. At a time when sectarian violence and political tension in Northern Ireland was at its zenith, Billy drove his family to one of the city's most troubled hotspots. Driving along the streets of the Republican gangland, he hurled abuse at the top of his voice and drunkenly invited retaliation. Such insensitivity was not only foolish but extremely dangerous. Nevertheless, it was the return journey that showed Mary just how radically her husband had changed. Instead of the kind and sensitive lad who had won her teenage heart, the terrified woman discovered that she was married to a callous and indifferent stranger. Careering down the road, Billy finally lost control of the car, hit a concrete barrier and ended up facing the opposite direction. Screaming hysterically, the children looked on in horror as the vehicle teetered on the brink of a dangerous drop. Incredulously, his family's safety was not Billy's first priority. Their fear and distress was secondary to his more immediate need. Leaving his wife and children sobbing, Billy fled the scene and headed for the nearest pub. Thankfully, the family managed to escape any serious injury and was driven home by a local woman who took pity on their plight.

As Mr James Leckie realised, without Christ at their helm, the Stevenson family were lost. With profound wisdom, the distinguished businessman continued to befriend the couple, winning their trust and pouring a measure of calm into their troubled lives. There was no doubt that as owner of Everton Engineering Company, he had been blessed with an abundance of wealth. Yet, like the Good Samaritan of scripture, when it came to binding the wounds of his fellow man, no cost was too great. Sensing an underlying craving for excitement as a contributing factor to Billy's drinking and gambling, James reckoned that a stimulating interest might prove a good alternative to the seductive powers of alcohol. When he proposed a series of flying lessons, Billy Stevenson was overwhelmed with surprise and gratitude. The older man's generosity and kindness may have provided his young friend with an insight into a world that did not revolve around drink, but it also allowed an unexpected glimpse of the principles of Christian love.

Initially, the flying lessons went well but, once on the ground, the trainee pilot continued to fill his life with the usual doses of pleasure. However, Mr Leckie remained undaunted and at every opportunity saturated Billy's ears as well as his heart with God's plan of salvation. Mary also benefited from the unexpected blessing in their lives. Very often the kindly benefactor would arrive at the Stevenson's door armed with messages of God's love and forgiveness as well as a huge bag of groceries. At every opportunity, their friend invited the couple to gospel meetings around the city. With a tasty fish supper beforehand, Billy often found it difficult to refuse!

On one occasion, the husband and wife, accompanied by James Leckie, arrived at Glenburn Gospel Hall to hear Mr Ben Sutton tell how God had saved and delivered him from the power of alcoholism. However, they almost missed the experience. With the hall packed to capacity, the trio received an apologetic explanation and politely turned away. Mary may have been disappointed but no doubt Billy heaved a huge sigh of relief. He had better things to do with his time. Thankfully, their friend refused to take no for an answer. Sensing that Billy's life was nearing crisis point, James Leckie was desperate to reach him. With the words, "it doesn't matter who comes out, these two are definitely going in!" he propelled the couple through the doors, up the aisle and into the only remaining space which, much to Billy's discomfort was right beside the platform. The young man didn't want to hear about the consequences of sin; neither did he want to confront his need of salvation. Billy's life had become so enmeshed in fringe organisations and trouble that there appeared to be no way out. What had begun as flirtatious curiosity rapidly snowballed as he turned toward the more sinister aspects of Northern Ireland's paramilitary groups. For many within the British Isles, 1971 brought nothing more complicated than the introduction of decimal currency. But, for the people of Northern Ireland, the year was stamped with bloodshed. Fuelled by alcohol, Billy Stevenson was among those carried along by a volatile wave of civil disturbance. As he sat in the crowded Gospel hall, Billy's thoughts were occupied, not by matters of eternity but how soon he could get back to his worldly pursuit of excitement.

At the end of the service, Jim Leckie asked if the couple would like to speak with Ben Sutton but Billy's negative reply was drowned by his wife's assurance that there was nothing she would like better. Seated at the back of the hall, they listened, Billy with mounting impatience, Mary with interest, while Ben Sutton spoke about Christ's work at Calvary. To his amazement, Billy heard his wife say that she wanted to have the certainty of salvation. While she had placed a childlike faith in Christ, the wife and mother needed the assurance of her sins forgiven. From that evening Mary Stevenson, placed her trust fully in the Lord and acknowledged Him as her Saviour. But his wife wasn't the only member of the family to trust Christ. Their young son, Billy junior, may have found his dad to be a poor role model in many ways. Yet, thankfully he had his paternal grandfather to show him, not only a better life, but the only way to find it. However, when Mr Stevenson senior led his grandson to the Lord he had no idea how God would eventually use the child to answer his lifetime of prayers.

As Mary's faith blossomed so did her joy. Circumstances hadn't changed, neither had her husband's attitude. Nevertheless, she had a peace that transcended all of life's problems. Desperate for her husband to share her happiness, Billy's name was at the top of his young wife's prayer list. However, it was Mary's mother and not her husband who was next in the family circle to accept Christ into her life. During yet another of Ben Sutton's messages, Mrs McMillan followed her daughter's example and gave her heart to the Lord. All around him, Billy could see Spirit of God at work. His family had found the peace and satisfaction that he desperately craved. Yet his life remained in turmoil. With a huge reservoir of patience, James Leckie refused to give up. At one time Billy's wreck of a car had driven his family toward death and destruction but it was his friend's sleek Mercedes that brought them to venues with a message of life. But regardless of the preacher's eloquent words, brilliant sermons or even a growing desire to understand, salvation continued to elude him. He could not grasp the simplicity of God's gift. Struggling and wrestling, Billy agreed to accompany Mr Leckie to a gospel meeting in Scrabo Hall, Newtownards where Derick Bingham was preaching the gospel. After the service, Billy continued to grapple with the thorny issues associated with his ungodly lifestyle. The situation in Northern Ireland had become increasingly dangerous. Organisations that he had so readily entered were no longer easy to leave. Any attempt to disengage would result in swift and severe penalties. Billy was faced with, not only the fear of eternity but a very real dread of life in the present. However, whatever advice he expected from Derick Bingham it was not the simple message he received. After listening to the Shankill Road man's tale of woe, the preacher had only one pearl of wisdom, "Get Christ first!"

The instruction was simple but, as far as Billy was concerned, it may as well have been rocket science! He knew the theory but could not translate it to everyday reality. When James Leckie brought him home, the kindly mentor endeavoured to explain and unfold the divine plan of salvation. However, Billy Stevenson's conversion wasn't to be James Leckie's harvest. The seed that was sown by godly parents was also ordained to be reaped from among the family circle. As Billy said goodnight to his friend and wearily climbed the stairs in search of sleep, his heart as well as his spirit was arrested by the prayers of his young son. Passing Billy junior's bedroom he heard the words, "Please save my daddy." The simplicity but sincerity of the child's plea pierced his conscience and pricked his heart, bringing tears to his eyes. Billy Stevenson had listened to many gifted speakers over the years but that evening, his little boy was the best he had ever heard. Immediately his fog of confusion was lifted as, with complete clarity, Billy suddenly understood God's message of salvation. Christ had already paid the price to set him free! Throwing himself upon the mercy of God, Billy Stevenson begged for forgiveness and, on 18th April 1971, surrendered his life to the Lord. Never before had Mary moved so quickly! Hearing her husband's shouts of joy, she dashed upstairs to enfold him in hugs of delight! Downstairs, James Leckie listened to the sounds of praise that God had brought to the Stevenson home. Quietly but with immense happiness, he left the little home to offer his individual prayer of thankfulness for the mighty work that God had done in the life of Billy Stevenson.

prompted Heavenly rejoicing but, there was no doubt that the little house in South Belfast was also filled with the sweet sound of praise and thanksgiving.

The weekend passed in a haze of family unity and joy but by Monday morning a cloud of apprehension had eclipsed a little of his happiness. Becoming a Christian had altered the direction of Billy's life. Yet, before he could embrace the future, he had to sever links with the past. Acquaintances and friends may have mourned the loss of a drinking buddy but local paramilitaries didn't relish the idea of losing a valuable recruit. Anxious but determined, Billy arrived at the organisation's headquarters eager to tender his resignation. There was no doubt that God had supplied him with the necessary courage but Billy was equally grateful for the provision of James Leckie's company. As he waited in his car outside, the Christian man prayed continually that his friend's reservoirs of strength be refilled.

Downstairs, the drinking saloon catered for those who sought to anesthetise the various pains of reality but on the first floor, a group of men gathered to hear their young member's request. With a secret knock, known only to those within the ranks, Billy waited permission to enter. He had no idea of the outcome but was certain that God would sustain him whatever happened. Looking round the assembled company, he took a deep breath and launched his plea. Regardless of harsh glares and sceptic glances, Billy Stevenson told of the divine love that refused to allow the buttresses of ignorance and sin to prevail. With a tremor in his voice, he recounted the story of Christ's pursuit of his soul and how, ultimately He proved impossible to resist. By the time he was finished, the room was cloaked in silence. One by one, the toughest and hardest men of the community lifted their eyes to meet his gaze. Reflected in each was a story of hopelessness as well as admiration. Although no-one voiced the collective thought, Billy knew that every individual envied his freedom as well as certainty of pardon. As he looked toward the chairman for a verdict, the new convert felt no sense of fear. While his level of involvement with the organisation had not led to any serious infractions of the law, the consequences of leaving the paramilitary arena could prove severe. Nevertheless, when weighed in the balance of serving God, the young man knew he could not maintain the association and was prepared for whatever punishment they decreed. Looking around the room, the leader of the group knew he had a silent assent to his decision. Quietly he turned to Billy and announced that, after listening to his testimony, everyone agreed that there would be no retribution. He was free to go. Bounding down the stairs, like a man reprieved, he rushed to the parked Mercedes and with praise, not to mention a huge portion of relief, excitedly shared the news with his friend.

While James Leckie was at one time responsible for Billy's interest in becoming a pilot, the older man was also instrumental in launching his preaching career. Barely a week after his salvation, the unlikely speaker found himself in the main role at a men's rescue mission. Terrified at the prospect of such a public responsibility, Billy offered inexperience and naivety to purchase escape. Refusing to brook any argument, James reminded his brother in Christ that, after a life time spent serving the devil, it was now time to obey his new Master! Despite his reluctance, the novice speaker took the platform and addressed the assembled men. Looking into the pitiful, unshaven faces, he suddenly recognised the same sense of despair and hopelessness that had once been the hallmark of his own life. Filled with a burning desire to reach those whom society had forgotten, Billy preached God's message of love and forgiveness with simplicity and truth. That evening, the young man's oratory skill may not have left an indelible impression but his sincerity, passion and ability to empathise touched many hearts. The event also ushered in an era of ministry to Billy's life. However, it also marked a change in the relationship between the new preacher and his mentor. With gentleness and honesty the businessman confessed that he did not have a gift for public speaking. His service lay in the quiet and personal field of individual evangelism. Nevertheless, another man waited to share the platform. Miraculously, his co-worker in the Lord would provide, not only years of knowledge and wisdom, but concern for the young man's personal, emotional and spiritual development. Selected from the unique arena of family love, Billy's latest mentor in Christ was his father.

From the moment Mary Stevenson was saved everything changed, including the colour of her hair! Instead of bleached blonde locks that she piled high in the latest 'beehive' fashion, the young mum returned to her less noticeable but more natural shades of mousey brown. Her husband's physical appearance may not have altered but Mary was convinced that Billy Stevenson was not the man she married. God had not given her an improved or updated version of the original model. He had blessed her with a completely new and better man. For the first time in her married life, Mary experienced a real sense of contentment and security. Instead of pubs and clubs, Billy spent his time enjoying the company of his family as well as the fellowship at Fortwilliam Gospel Hall where, just four weeks after he had accepted Christ, both he and Mary wife were baptized.

By this stage, the Stevenson family had exchanged their terraced home with its draughty outside toilet for the luxury of one with an indoor bathroom as well as three sizeable bedrooms. Situated in the Highfield Estate area of West Belfast the housing development was to enjoy a reputation for more than modern accommodation. Known as a Loyalist stronghold the neighbourhood had, over the decades, proved a venue for everything from dawn swoops by security forces to unexpected Presidential visits from South East Asia. Whatever VIP, Xanana Gusamo from East Timor made of the hilly avenues and rugged community during his whistle stop tour, is a mystery. But, no doubt neither the authorities nor the President were aware of the talent or treasure that had been hidden among the pebble dashed semi-detached houses. Olympic medallist, Wayne McCullough, grew up in the area and would one day earn his reputation as Northern Ireland's 'Pocket Rocket' of the boxing world. Billy and Mary Stevenson's future role in the life of a Korean orphan was equally hidden.

Mr Leckie continued to feature prominently in the young couple's life, guiding, teaching and encouraging them on their journey of faith. But gradually, his divine purpose served, he withdrew to the more natural periphery of the Stevenson's circle of friends. In his place, Billy's father took on the job of spiritual adviser and companion, a role he had desired from his son's arrival in the world.

outnumber other less sombre occasions for church gatherings. Ministers and pastors were weighed down by the weight of their duties and the sorrow of their congregations. 1972 went on record as the worst of the troubled era with a record for the highest number of fatalities. Frustration and anger led to sporadic outbursts of civil disturbance. Crowds gathered to protest at perceived injustices. Sometimes, the incidents were confined to harsh words and an exchange of sectarian slander but very often bullets were the chosen method of communication.

At one time, Billy Stevenson was among those who tossed insults as well as bricks. However, as a saved man, his missives were taken from the Word of God and coated with the sweet balm of forgiveness and love. On one occasion, the young preacher found that his gospel message of eternal life coincided with society's missiles of death and destruction. As he took the platform at Old Park Gospel Hall, situated in the working class quarter of North Belfast, Billy was aware of a gun battle erupting outside the building. Standing under the podium light, he looked out over a sea of expectant but slightly nervous faces. As the bullets ricocheted off the walls, Billy detected a ripple of restless anxiety amongst his listeners. As he watched, the congregation began, one by one, to crouch beside their seats. Even Mary and Billy's mum had adopted a safer, less conspicuous position! Eventually one of the elders indicated to another brother that it would be wise to douse all the lights except one. The only illumination left intact was over the podium and above Billy's head! Framed in a halo of a golden glow, the young speaker was visible to both his listeners as well as the terrorists! Unsure whether to abandon his text and hide behind the pulpit, Billy decided to trust his safety to God and continued. Amidst the noise of the gun battle, he sounded a message of hope, although there's no doubt that is was proclaimed in a slightly tremulous and wobbly tone.

Accompanied by his father, Billy toured the various gospel halls, both in the city as well as more rural locations. However, in the days following his salvation, it was a trip to town with his mother that proved a memorable event for the young man. Growing up in a Christian home, Billy was aware of, not only God's Word, but the men who preached His message. Among servants like Harry Andrews, Ben Sutton, the Howarth family and Frank Knox, he had heard his parents speak highly of James Flanigan. As soon as her son had accepted Christ, Mrs Stevenson lost no time in spreading the news. Taking him to the Belfast Co-operative Society in the heart of Belfast's city, she introduced him to Mr Flanigan. In the grand scheme of things such an event may have appeared insignificant but to Billy Stevenson, it was a privilege to share his testimony of God's grace and mercy with such men. As it slowly dawned on him that he had been the object of many sincere and tender prayers, he felt greatly blessed as well as humbled.

   While the Stevenson family continued to worship at the Fortwilliam fellowship, their daily environment became increasingly dangerous. Crime as well as terrorist activity in the area was on the increase and James Leckie grew fearful for their safety. He thought that it might be easier for them as well as safer if the couple moved to one of the more peaceful areas outside the city. During a visit, he told Mary and Billy of a lovely new development that was under construction in the suburban town of Glengormley, about six miles from Belfast. The couple, despite enthusiastic interest, confessed that the expensive deposit required for such a move was well beyond their means. Nevertheless, they agreed to go and look at the new development. Mary fell in love with the little plot of land that promised not only a beautiful three bed-roomed home, but a garden where the children could play and she and Billy could relax on warm summer evenings. Sensing her appreciation, James Leckie made a handsome suggestion. If the couple could afford the mortgage repayments, he would give them the necessary deposit! With Billy's regular job at the British Oxygen Company plus Mary's salary from the bakery, their dream home was definitely affordable. Within a few months, the family was enjoying life in middle class suburbia. Sharing a cup of tea as well as a chuckle, Mary often remarked that, at one time, being surrounded by so many policemen as neighbours would have given Billy a severe bout of indigestion!

   Gradually, life settled to a comfortable and predictable routine. The children adapted well to the nearby school while Billy's job provided them with an enjoyable, comfortable lifestyle. However, although Mary loved her new home, she continued to hanker after the familiarity of the close knit community that is peculiar to Belfast's Shankill Road. Glengormley was a pleasant little town but she missed the open, busy and intimate atmosphere of her old neighbourhood. The suburban housing estate, although smarter and cleaner, lacked the friendly and, at times, nosey intrusiveness of her Shankill neighbours. As often as possible, she took a bus into Belfast's City Centre followed by another to her parent's home in Disraeli Street just off the beloved 'Road' and revelled in the luxury of a strong pot of tea, a chat and huge dose of laughter. At the time, two bus journeys seemed a long way from home but she had no idea just how far God would eventually take her.

As Billy continued to study and learn from God's Word, his preaching skill increased. Slowly but surely the Lord was preparing him for service. Mary was also being groomed for a new way of life. However, her talents lay in a more domestic realm. Initially, the significance of a few cookery lessons appeared little more than a welcome variation to the family menu and an enjoyable interest for the mother of two. But in the coming years, the family would appreciate Mary's ability to turn a few measly ingredients into a hearty meal.

Mary's introduction into the world of basic but tasty treats began when, after inviting James Leckie for dinner, she served a roast that appeared mutilated rather than carved. Cooking nutritious, wholesome or even tasty meals for her family had never been a priority. Mary had too many other things demanding her attention. After all, there was little point in providing dinner for a husband who either didn't come home or was too drunk to notice what he ate. Her mother had experienced a similar problem. Getting through the day was more important than baking buns. There was no room in life for such trivialities. For too long their life had been orchestrated by the immediate and urgent demands of simple necessity. Nevertheless, as James Leckie looked on in horror at the hacked offering, his heart melted. His young friends had been deprived of so many things that he had taken for granted. Yet, regardless of their lack, the couple had managed to contribute a few gems to his own storehouse of wealth. Throughout their friendship, Mary and Billy had demonstrated the precious and sometimes undervalued gift of laughter. Tentatively and with great diplomacy he retrieved one such nugget and asked, "Mary did you happen to use a hatchet to carve this joint?" Erupting in laughter, the whole family acknowledged that the said instrument was Mary's favourite cooking utensil! A few days later, Mr Leckie's sister arrived, armed with recipes, flour, butter, eggs and every ingredient necessary to turn Mary into a dab hand at 'wee buns', cakes, curries and many other delights that tempted her family's taste buds. As the women weighed, measured, kneaded and whipped their way toward culinary perfection, they also created a firm bond of friendship. With flour everywhere, they chatted and giggled, adding a huge amount of pleasure to Mary's day, not to mention the Stevenson's dinner table. In a few short years, the true value of these lessons would finally come to light and Mary would thank God for His provision and care for even the smallest detail.

Chapter 6
THE CALL TO SERVICE

INSTEAD OF fractured dreams and broken hearts, the Stevenson's life was suddenly filled with contentment and hope. Billy's job with the British Oxygen Company was well paid while Mary's extra hours at a local fresh fish shop boosted the household income and helped pay for necessities like school uniforms and new shoes. At one time cigarettes and alcohol had taken priority over Billy's daily bread never mind his children's growing feet. But along with eternal security, salvation brought peace and stability to the Stevenson home.

While Mary perfected her homemaking skills and experimented with recipes for 'shepherd's pie' and 'vegetable broth,' her husband laboured over his preaching technique. The mid seventies had not yet ushered in an era of peace. Northern Ireland was still in the grip of political upheaval and violence. Nevertheless, the Province was blessed by a wealth of gifted and able preachers. From little gatherings on street corners to Pastor Willie Mullan, Mr David Craig of Ballymena, the Paisley brothers as well as Hedley Murphy's outreach missions, the people of Ulster enjoyed many anointed ministries. Presenting the gospel is a wonderful privilege but it also carries a great weight of responsibility. However, Billy learned a valuable lesson fairly early in his preaching career. Frank Knox, one of the most respected speakers of his generation taught him that oratory skill has absolutely nothing to do with winning souls!

The lesson began when Billy, after preaching the gospel message, stepped off the platform at Ormeau Road Gospel Hall in South Belfast and was intercepted by the well known and forthright brother. Nervously, the young, inexperienced preacher toyed with his tie while Mr Knox's gaze pinned him to the spot. Beginning at Billy's well polished shoes and travelling the length of his crease free suit, the older man silently scrutinised every inch. Curious as to the problem, Billy's thoughts immediately flew to his sermon. Was it too short, too long, or perhaps the delivery had been all wrong? Finally Frank Knox looked into the younger man's anxious eyes and solemnly pronounced that the error lay with Billy's trousers! 'There's no hole in the knees!' he barked. Immediately Billy understood. It wasn't that Mr Knox was advocating a wardrobe that was in urgent and constant need of mending. Simply but profoundly, the experienced man of God revealed that the secret of a powerful ministry was prayer. In order to preach with divine power it was essential to kneel in the presence of God until trouser legs were, metaphorically, in shreds.

The routine of family life and assembly fellowship continued. Mary had grown accustomed to the journey into Belfast and was soon hopping on and off the buses with ease. Her mum's salvation shortly after her own provided not only delight, but an extra dimension to the maternal bond. Along with recipes, the two women shared everything from current events to the latest supermarket bargains. Armed with a cup of tea and a 'Paris Bun,' one of the O'Hara Bakery's sponge and sugar delights, they chuckled over Billy junior's escapades or his sister's childish antics. Their conversation, interspersed with words of praise and thanksgiving, wove the happy pattern of life and sparkled with luminous threads of gold.

As his wife matured and developed in her Christian faith, Billy was also beginning to experience a new element to his relationship with God. A burning desire to see others brought to Christ began to consume the preacher's mind and heart. However, Billy's thoughts reached far beyond the confines of Northern Ireland's gospel halls. He knew that, despite its problems, his country already enjoyed an abundance of divine messengers. Other nations were not so privileged. Across the world, people, blinded by sin and bound by poverty knew nothing of God's mercy and love. Slowly but surely, compassion for these lost and hopeless individuals, ignited a fire in Billy's heart. As he learned of cultures where communist regimes or religious dogma instigated fear and curtailed freedom, the Belfast man longed to bring them the news of God's salvation. Before long, the burden for people of foreign lands was occupying every waking moment. Yet, regardless of his enthusiasm and passion, there was none more aware than Billy Stevenson of his limited abilities. He knew he did not have the gift to teach or unravel the intricacies of divine doctrine. His oratory skill possessed an honest simplicity but he was not one of life's natural speakers. Nevertheless, he had experienced the life changing power of the Almighty God. Billy Stevenson knew and loved the Lord Jesus and he wanted others to do the same.

Meeting John Anderson, a missionary stationed in Korea, was like putting a torch to dry kindling! Despite a couple of failed attempts to arrange a meeting, Billy finally caught up with the man of God during a furlough in Belfast. When the gospel meeting had finished, John took Billy to his home and, pointing to a huge map on the wall, indicated the enormous areas of need throughout Korea. Overwhelmed with compassion, Billy was moved by the incredible scale of the regions. His instinct may have been to catch the first available flight to the Korean capital and tell them of God's mercy but he needed divine direction. He also needed to tell his wife!

Weeks and months of heart searching and prayer followed. At times, missionary work appeared the only direction possible. Yet, the comfortable trappings of home proved an able seductress. After years of instability and uncertainty, Billy was finally able to provide his family with a sense of normality and comfort. His wife could shop without mentally calculating the cost of a couple of lamb chops. His kids, with their shiny shoes and new uniforms blended well with suburban school society. How could he even think of robbing them of a lifestyle they so richly deserved? Surely he had caused enough chaos without taking them on a journey whose destination he could not predict?

Nonetheless, Billy was certain that God was calling him. Regardless of the reasons, logistics or arguments, he knew that his life was not his own. He had been bought with a price that transcended everything. When weighed in the balance, Christ's sacrifice demanded obedience. Slowly and imperceptibly, Billy's prayer began to adopt the attitude of 'where' rather than 'if.' He knew without a shadow of a doubt that God was directing him toward the mission field. His only request was that the Lord would take him to a nation that required the simplicity of the gospel message. With no desire for acclaim or reputation, Billy's only concern was to rescue those on their way to a lost eternity. After speaking with John Anderson, the people of Korea had become uppermost in his mind. All he needed was God's command to go.

Attuned to her husband's moods, Mary knew that divine concerns occupied his heart. She had been privy to his prayers and understood that God was calling him to a new field of service. However, the prospect of leaving her lovely new home as well as settled lifestyle was not something that filled her with eager anticipation. Yet, she was not left aimless and without direction. As she began to read the story of Abraham and Sarah, Mary discovered that, regardless of where God called her husband, it was her duty as well as service to follow. Despite her misgivings, she would support Billy and seek God for the personal sense of comfort and reassurance she craved.

Billy's confirmation that he was going to Korea arrived in the early hours of the morning as he travelled along a lonely country road near the border town of Newry. Seized by a sense of urgency, and in desperate need of assurance, he pulled into a lay-by and, while the world slept, poured out his troubled heart in prayer. With a rural orchestra of birdsong ringing in his ears, he presented his desires, passions, shortcomings and fears at the eternal Throne of Grace. Acknowledging confusion as well as concern, he confessed his complete inadequacy for the task. Nevertheless, he also pledged his willingness to obey. If God wanted him in Korea, he would go. As an incredible sense of peace flooded his heart, Billy turned to the gospel of Luke, chapter 24 verses 45-49, and read his family's future. With a vow to open the people's eyes that they might understand the scripture, God promised Billy Stevenson a rich harvest of souls. Pulling onto the road, Billy made his way home to tell Mary that their time in suburbia was limited. God was taking them on a new adventure. He knew their destination was the poverty stricken streets of Korea. The only question was when.

Chapter 7
PREPARATIONS

INITIALLY, MARY and Billy hugged the secret of God's call between them. Telling no-one they waited for Him to build the bridge that would lead them safely from one culture to another. As each obstacle arose, they quietly committed it to divine counsel, and with stepping stones of grace the husband and wife moved slowly but with certainty toward their future destination.

As with all major undertakings, the first problem Mary and Billy encountered was finance. Determined that they would burden neither their assembly fellowship nor Korean society, they asked God to provide a buyer for their home. With the proceeds from the sale of the house they would have more than enough to meet any initial and immediate expenses. To the causal observer, there was no indication that the Glengormley property had entered the housing market. While the area exhibited a rash of brightly coloured 'for sale' notices to entice prospective buyers, the Stevenson's garden was adorned with nothing more interesting than a few flower beds and a couple of leafy shrubs. Leaving the matter before the Throne of Grace, Billy and Mary carried on with the business of life and waited quietly for an answer to their prayer. Both knew that, when the time was right, God would solve the financial situation by providing the perfect purchaser for their home.

As well as the usual outbreaks of civil disturbance, by 1973, many in Northern Ireland had experienced the misery of 'eviction' from their home. Fuelled by mistrust and anxiety, Protestant and Catholic neighbours forgot their previous ability to live in happy co-existence. Memories of friendships bonded by poverty instead of religion were submerged in the stormy seas of suspicion and political disarray. Ignoring the majority's voice of reason, many communities succumbed to irrational fears of bigotry or the threat of intimidation and demanded that those of an opposing religion leave the area. All over the Province, tears of sorrow as well as shame flowed at the loss of neighbours who, over the years, had earned the status of friend. For some, the links spanned many generations and severing them proved a painful and difficult wrench.

Mary's boss was one such victim. Forced to abandon his home, the Catholic businessman and his young family was in desperate need of accommodation. Upset and shocked by the experience, he was eager to find a calmer, less troubled area in which to raise his children. With its reputation for mixed and middle class housing developments, Glengormley seemed the ideal haven. The Troubles, confined mainly to inner city Belfast had not invaded the busy suburban town to the same degree, making it a popular residential location for young families. Realising that one of his employees lived in the area, the supermarket manager decided to ask if she knew of any in the estate that was currently for sale. The full impact of the situation was not lost on Mary. She immediately recognised the divine handprint on such an unusual query and couldn't wait to tell Billy. However, her husband's reaction to news of her employer's dilemma, tempered any undue excitement. Patiently he explained that they should do nothing to encourage the man's interest or build his hopes. Instead, they would continue to wait and allow God's purposes to unfold.

However, when Mary's boss, accompanied by his wife and children arrived on the Stevenson's doorstep and asked if they would be willing to sell their property, God's signpost proved impossible to ignore. Still Billy hesitated. Inviting the little group into his home, he explained an additional though unusual clause to any potential contract. If the man was serious about becoming the next owner of the Glengormley property, he would have to purchase more than just bricks and mortar. When Billy and Mary left their home, they intended to travel light. Apart from their clothes, the only thing they would take to their new life would be memories. Every stick of furniture as well as carpets, curtains, crockery and cutlery would remain in the house. Whatever the businessman's wife thought of living in a place where another woman's taste and style dictated décor and furniture is unknown but, no doubt, she appreciated the timeless appeal and quality of Augher Castle's antique tables and chairs. As owner of the historic residence, Mr Leckie's gifts had, at one time, added a touch of luxury and splendour to the Stevenson's home. Yet, as well as comfort for his friends, perhaps the handsome pieces helped sway the prospective buyers. Or maybe it was merely desperation to find a suitable and available property that led the couple to agree to Billy's terms. Whatever the reason, there is no doubt that the little family's presence in the Stevenson's house was orchestrated by God. After looking around and admiring everything, the family readily accepted the unusual conditions. The sale was agreed. God had provided the means to take the Stevenson family to Korea but by the time the deal was finalised, the couple had received more than a monetary blessing. They had learned a valuable lesson in faith. Trusting God to provide a buyer for their home had indeed required patience. Nevertheless, the wait for an answer to prayer had been cushioned by the luxury of comfortable surroundings. It did not prove so easy in the midst of squalor and poverty but at that moment in time, as Mary and Billy offered their thanks and praise for God's wonderful provision, they had no idea of the trials that waited.

When Mr Leckie heard of Billy's call to Korea, he was delighted. In contrast, Mary's mum was devastated by the news. Like many women of her generation, Mrs McMillan regarded any destination within a hundred mile radius of Belfast as 'foreign'. At over five thousand miles away, South Korea might as well have been on another planet! Her husband, while not as emotionally demonstrative as his wife, was just as upset at the prospect of losing an entire branch of his family. As far as Mary's dad was concerned, the idea of taking two young children half way round the world and introducing them to a strange language and alien culture was complete madness. Apart from their own sense of loss, the distraught grandparents feared for their loved ones welfare and safety. Mr McMillan's knowledge of Korea may have been limited but he knew that it entailed a much harsher way of life.

Aware of their confusion and heartache, Mary did her best to explain, comfort and reassure. She parried their arguments and pleading with honest simplicity. Billy Stevenson had been called to bring hope to many who walked in darkness and, as his wife, she would go with him. While Mary had no idea what the future held, she was certain that God could meet all their needs.

As the days passed and preparations got underway, Mary's visits to her parent's home became a collection of bitter sweet memories. Acutely aware that their time

LEAVING BELFAST

IN MAY 1974, the people of Northern Ireland woke to cold showers and uncooked breakfasts. Those depending on public transport rapidly discovered that, as well as electricity supplies, buses and trains were also off the menu. Within a few days, barricades of burning cars ensured that city streets and country roads alike were equally impassable. Before long the breakdown of the Province's social infrastructure had spread to include waste management. Gathered in rotting piles, thousands of black plastic bags spilled their contents along roads and pavements, polluting the air and marring the normally picturesque landscape. In fact the only thing that remained in abundant supply was intimidation imposed by paramilitary gangs of teenage thugs and masked men. Like a scene from some Hollywood horror movie, life in Northern Ireland ground to a halt. Yet, instead of an invasion by aliens, the catastrophe occurred when a few local politicians used their influence to oppose a power sharing executive. With an outcry of incredulous disbelief, they fanned the flames of community insecurity, anger and frustration. Ian Paisley and his colleagues were among those who advocated that Ulster refuse to accept the current political solution. With impassioned rhetoric, he and his associates highlighted the adverse consequences of the democratically elected government and within two weeks of the Ulster Unionist Action Council strike, any suggestion of Unionists sharing authority with Nationalists was completely destroyed and Northern Ireland remained under direct rule from Westminster. Little did anyone realise that, thirty three years later, the Province would adopt a more inclusive attitude. Ironically, Mr Paisley would assume the role of Northern Ireland's First Minister with Martin McGuinness, from the hardline Republican community, serving as his deputy.

Nevertheless, in 1974, political compromises as well as future solutions remained in the realms of mystery. As far as Billy and Mary Stevenson were concerned, the events of daily life were just another stepping stone toward a new field of service. Yet, perhaps the unexpected deprivation of modern luxuries provided a sneak preview of the life to come! The Ulster Unionist Action Council strike may have been founded on political principles but the subsequent reality was a foretaste of Korean normality for the Stevenson family.

Eventually, preparations for departure were complete. Mary and Billy had sold their home as well as its furnishings, their one way tickets to Korea were purchased and they were ready to go were God called. As 8th June 1974 dawned, Mary Stevenson's heart trembled with a mixture of fear, excitement and an overwhelming sense of sadness. Cocooned in the shadows of early morning stillness, she snuggled against the comforting warmth of her husband and tried to prepare for the day ahead. In a few hours, she would leave everything that was familiar and precious to embark on a journey she could not yet envisage. Mary Stevenson had never travelled outside of Northern Ireland and the prospect of boarding an aeroplane filled her with terror! In the quiet solitude of half light, the young woman prayed silently for strength. Regardless of her conviction that her place was with Billy, leaving her mother, father and siblings, not to mention sailing through clouds at fantastic speeds, seemed a feat beyond natural endurance.

No doubt, in the next room, Mary's parents found sleep equally elusive. Whatever hope they had entertained for their daughter and son-in-law's change of heart, had long since fled. The next few hours would bring a few shy, inadequate words of love, a hurried embrace, and a final farewell. With five thousand miles between them, Mary's mum and dad realised the impossibility of frequent visits. They understood that the next time they saw their grandchildren, Isabelle and William junior would have lost the soft contours of childhood. Like all devoted grandparents, Mr and Mrs McMillan did not want to miss a single moment of their loved ones lives. They wanted to remain a part of their daily experiences, share in the laughter, commiserate with disappointment and offer the guiding hand of experience. As they dwelt on the consequences of the day ahead, their sense of loss proved akin to grief. Billy's parents, although equally saddened by the young family's imminent departure, understood their son's desire to follow where God led. After years of familiarity with scriptural giants like Abraham, Moses, Joshua and David, they recognised the importance of obedience. Nevertheless, the knowledge did not provide an emotional balm. It is never easy to say goodbye to those we love.

As the sun tore its way through Belfast's cloudy morning, Mr James Leckie's Mercedes had one more journey to perform in the life of William and Mary Stevenson. The sleek, silent and comfortable vehicle had, at one time, kept a patient vigil outside Belfast's clubs and pubs, waiting to bring an inebriated husband home to his family. It had also taken its reluctant passenger to hear the Word of God preached and expounded at the various gospel halls across the Province. Then, when the light of mercy and grace had dawned on his soul, the same beautiful car had transported Billy Stevenson to venues where other perishing souls waited to hear God's message of pardon and mercy. For three years it had played a dominant role in affording transport for the young family to worship at their local assembly in Fortwilliam Gospel Hall.

But on 8th June 1974, it was Mr James Leckie who had the privilege of driving Billy and his family on their final journey in Northern Ireland. With the sale of their home, the Stevensons had spent their remaining hours with Mary's parents in Disraeli Street, in the working class area of West Belfast. When James Leckie arrived to take the little group to Belfast's International Airport, even he was surprised by the neighbourly display of emotion. Locals lined the long, winding pavement to say goodbye to one of their own. Many had known Mary since childhood, had shared in the celebration of her marriage, commiserated with her in the grief of maternal loss and empathised with the distress of an alcoholic husband. Equally, although without understanding, they had expressed delight at news of her salvation. Yet, few could appreciate the desire to abandon recently gained comforts of job security and material ease for a life of uncertainty. Nonetheless, they had glimpsed a little of the power that had transformed an unhappy and insecure family into a stable and thriving unit.

Calling out their good wishes for future happiness and prosperity, neighbours cheerfully said goodbye but, faced with the sad although stoic countenance of her dad, a hot and searing pain pierced Mary's heart. As she bade him farewell, the heartbroken father challenged his daughter with God's providential care. With the words, "We'll see if your God provides for you now," Mr McMillan watched as Mary climbed into the Mercedes and headed toward a new life. The sentiments were to echo far into the future but, as both Mary and her father were to learn, God is ever faithful. With a touch of kindness, James Leckie proffered a final piece of advice that, from the days of ancient scripture has proven wise. Touching her hand he told his young friend, "Don't look back."

The scene at the airport was no different to that of Mary's home. Rarely had the departure lounge of the Belfast International Airport been so full of well wishers. Crowds, from Mary and Billy's assembly fellowship as well as individual friends and family members had gathered to offer their prayers, support and encouragement. Among them was Billy's Aunt Margaret, the woman he describes as a 'prayer warrior.' It was she who had first approached Mr Leckie on behalf of her alcoholic and unhappy nephew. Whatever her feelings on the morning of Billy's departure remain a mystery but, no doubt, she added a word of thanksgiving for the salvation of the young man who, as the object of divine mercy, was about to embark on a wonderful service for God.

Finally the flight was called and Mary and Billy, amidst a flurry of hasty embraces and floods of tears, bade their farewell. Boarding the plane that was initially bound for London, Mary succumbed to a fit of terror! Gripping the seat, she remained pale faced and white knuckled for the remainder of the short trip. As far as the Shankill Road woman was concerned, going to live amongst people of a different language and culture seemed like 'wee buns' compared to travelling thousands of feet above ground in what appeared little more than a tin can! But then, Mary had a lot to learn about her new life. Six weeks later, she would gladly travel in any form of transport just to get home to the familiarity of the Shankill Road and a cup of tea with her mum.

Chapter 9
ARRIVING AT SEOUL
ॐ

WITH THE Sea of Japan crashing along its Eastern shores and the Yellow Sea lapping at the Western side of its sandy coves, South Korea lies at the Southernmost tip of the Korean peninsula. Surrounded by mountains, most of the terrain cannot sustain its population with an arable livelihood. The climate may be described as 'temperate' but compared to the soft drizzle of Northern Ireland's intermittent summer showers, South Korea's rainy season known as 'jangma' can prove an unrelenting downpour. Late summer typhoons and bitterly cold winters, may have been an unwanted but acceptable forecast for much of Asian society. But to the couple from Belfast's Shankill Road, it seemed anything but mild!

Known as both the 'Land of Morning Calm' and the 'Hermit Kingdom,' Korea's national and cultural identity spans over five thousand years. From 1392 until 1910 it was governed by Confucian scholars who believed that worldly authority was conferred only by a heavenly mandate. However, this dynastic authority known as 'Yi' was abolished in 1910 when the Japanese Emperor stated in his 'Imperial Prescript' that all Koreans should be treated as subjects of Japan. The ensuing colonial government was made up of Japanese military leaders who lost no time in exercising their judicial, legislative and administrative power. The pursuit of a ruthless policy that suppressed the expression of both speech and cultural heritage, rapidly led to the loss of Korea's individuality and identity. Before long, Japanese had replaced the national Korean language on the country's school curriculum.

Eventually, the outbreak of war in 1950 brought total devastation to the people of both Korea's Communist controlled North and her Capitalist neighbours in the South. By 27th July 1953, an agreement signed by the USA, China, as well as South and North Korea, ended hostilities by creating a four mile wide demilitarized zone along the border. However, the creation, in many experts' opinion, was to prove the world's most dangerous flashpoint. In fact forty year's later, American President, Bill Clinton would describe the area as, "the scariest place on earth."

By the time it appeared on the Stevenson family's horizon, Korea was still in a state of post war shock. Apart from the loss of three hundred thousand civilians, the county's social structure was torn and fragmented. Countless orphans, widows and seriously injured servicemen crammed the streets of the capital city of Seoul, searching for loved ones or simply a piece of their shattered lives. With sixty per cent of its industrial cities destroyed South Korea was particularly affected by the plummeting economy and hope was as scarce as material commodities.

After three nerve wrecking flights, the Stevenson family arrived at their destination. Billy, well used to all forms of travel since his days with the military forces, had no problem with any mode of transportation. The children overcome by excitement and a sense of adventure, regarded the event as nothing short of magical. Their mother was not so fortunate. From the moment she boarded the initial flight to London until the pilot announced their arrival in Korea, Mary had remained tight lipped and white faced the entire journey. But regardless of how each individual member of the Stevenson family coped with aviation travel, when the plane finally landed on Korean soil, they all shared a common complaint. Billy, his wife and two children were completely shattered! Never before had they known such an extreme sense of fatigue. Neither had they experienced such intense heat. Emerging from the aircraft, the Northern Irish missionaries were blasted with the full force of Asian sunshine. Their welcome from South Korean as well as European brothers and sisters in Christ was equally overpowering.

Rushing onto the tarmac, the delighted believers showered the family with words of welcome as well as bouquets of flowers. More used to the reserved attitude of an Ulster heritage, Mary and Billy were stunned by the overt display of emotion. Nevertheless, both were equally delighted and pleased. Yet, when one of the brothers, Mr Eddie James, took them to spend the night at his home, the couple couldn't help but long for the cooler atmosphere of their Irish abode! Instead of the familiarity of small and sometimes frigidly cold rooms, the young family was shown to a chamber that was stiflingly hot. Some Belfast householders may have complained about draughty windows that rattled in their frames but Mary and Billy would have welcomed the extra bit of ventilation! Eddie James, concerned lest his guests from the Northern hemisphere find the Korean evenings a little chilly, had heaped an abundance of blankets and duvets on their beds. Somehow, the fact that June until August, the country was at its hottest, seemed to have escaped his notice. By the time dawn arrived, Mary was certain that their Korean accommodation had worked better than any previous diet. She must have lost pounds in perspiration!

The next day, the family began to explore. There wasn't much about her new home that Mary Stevenson liked. The sights, sounds but particularly the smells of Seoul's city streets were totally alien to her Northern Irish culture. In 1974 the Province of Ulster still wrestled with serious issues of political instability and violence but as Mary wistfully reminisced, it did at least enjoy a modern drainage system! Within a few weeks of renting a house in the one of Seoul's poorest areas, the family was initiated into several of the less agreeable community practices. Every week, a foul stench permeated the air as dry toilets were removed from individual homes and emptied by crew from the local council. The stomach churning smells seemed to cling to both furnishings and clothing from one week until the next. Apart from sewage collection problems, Mary found the obligation to collect a monthly portion of rat poison from the Town Hall, equally upsetting. Vermin, that appeared better fed than the people, ran and scuttled throughout the hilly streets, burrowing between the walls of individual homes and taking advantage of every available nook and cranny. Sharing her life with the destitute was one thing but Mary had never envisaged the need to share her living space with a bunch of totally ungrateful rodents!

However, for the Belfast woman, it was Korean cuisine that proved most unpalatable. Buried parcels of rotting cabbage combined with hot and spicy peppers did little for the sense of smell never mind the taste buds. Plates of rice may have been more acceptable but not when served at breakfast as well as lunch and dinner! Vegetables that had to be exhumed before eating or bland offerings of rice played havoc with the digestive system but when local butchers offered choice cuts of dog instead of lamb, Mary's homesickness arrived at approximately the same speed her appetite fled. Yet it wasn't only Mary who found the difference in cultural appetites upsetting. Poor William junior, also encountered an unforgettable misery when, after trusting his recently acquired pet to a neighbour's care, found that the little dog had ended up on the Korean's family menu! For weeks, the lad was inconsolable at the memory of his loss. Nevertheless, throughout those early clashes of culture, God provided a soothing balm of divine comfort to ease the shock of distressed and fretting souls. Gradually, Mary and her family grew accustomed to the nauseating smells, and strange practices. Yet, there remained many instances when homesickness surfeited and Mary, gazing at a lone aeroplane in the broad expanse of Asian sky, wished she were on board and headed for home.

While his wife and children tried to adapt to their new environment, Billy immediately set about preaching the gospel message. With the aid of another brother's interpretation skill, he visited local assemblies, expounding God's message of salvation as well as offering words of exhortation and encouragement. Touched by the warmth of the reception, Billy felt both humbled and privileged. Eager to reach as many as possible he journeyed, heedless of distance, from village to village, sharing the wonderful news of God's love and mercy.

Soon, the couple had opened their home where, as well as Bible study with a few Korean believers, Mary began to introduce women and children to the Lord. Seated in her tiny living room, surrounded by a crowd of laughing, dark eyed youngsters, the young mother was at her happiest. Her maternal love combined with a ready smile and a sense of fun made Mrs Stevenson popular with kids of all ages. Apart from a natural affinity with children, one of Mary's greatest assets in securing their trust was the couple's friendship with an elderly man called Harabudji. Well known by his community, the kindly figure was adopted by local kids as a sort of honorary grandfather and respected his judgement. Very often, with a torch lighting his path, he scoured the foothills of the mountain, calling for little ones to make their way to the 'foreigners' home where they'd be sure to find a warm welcome and maybe a bite to eat. They'd also hear some fantastic stories about the heroes and giants that lived long ago. More importantly, they would learn of a man called Jesus who loved all the children of the world. For young lives acquainted with poverty and bereft of affection, such a promise brought a warm glimmer of hope.

Apart from the old man's friendliness toward the Stevenson family, it was his ability to speak English that delighted the Irish 'foreigners.' Having worked at an American army camp based in Korea, Harabudji had picked up enough English language skills to allow a decent conversation. Starved of a proper cup of tea as well as her mother tongue, Mary relished every opportunity for a chat. There was no doubt that the Stevenson family suffered a severe bout of culture shock. Everything about their new environment was unfamiliar and different to anything they'd ever known. Mary in particular found the pangs of homesickness overwhelming but, the first time she visited Harabudji's home, their rented house no longer seemed like such a hovel. Instead of four walls to keep out the elements, the elderly man's abode was a hole dug into the side of the mountain and his door, a plastic sheet held in place by bricks and stones. Yet, regardless of their friend's material lack, he had an abundant supply of hospitality and kindness. At every visit, he insisted the Stevenson family share a cup of tea although, to Mary, the obnoxious liquid tasted nothing like the tea bag version of home!

Yet, it wasn't only the Stevenson family who found their presence in Korea a strange and, at times, disorientating experience. Their neighbours were equally curious about the new arrivals. No doubt the family provided a novel topic for conversation. Their motive for exchanging the comforts of Western prosperity and economic growth in order to live in comparative poverty seemed inconceivable. While their husbands discussed the politics of the family's presence, their wives were more interested by Mary's wardrobe. The long woollen skirts proved a constant source of amusement as the Korean ladies seized every opportunity to follow the newcomer, eager to inspect and touch the unfamiliar material. At first Mary countered their curiosity with a gentle but firm rebuff but in the end decided it was quicker and easier to simply stand still and allow them to inspect her attire. Trips to the shops began to include a little extra 'inspection' time.

Whatever the women made of the newcomer's fashion sense, it was her hairstyle that caused most problems. Despite Mary's attempt to explain her desire for what she affectionately called a 'Brethren Pleat,' the local hair stylist had no idea what her customer wanted. With exaggerated actions, Mary tried to convey the basics of back combing hoping that the woman would grasp the concept and fold her hair into a neat and modest pleat. Unfortunately, the hair stylist's imagination and skill didn't reach beyond the back combing stage. After washing her client's hair with rainwater, she set

Chapter 10
THE DISCOVERY

WITH WARM balmy days and the scent of apple blossom in the air, April and May are reputedly the most beautiful months in the Korean calendar. The summer sun makes June and July uncomfortably hot but by August the heat is unbearable. Although there's always the torrential downpours of Asia's rainy season to provide a welcome but drenching shower! As the seasonal clock moves toward winter, temperatures may be equally extreme but the landscape is just as picturesque. Snow covered mountains as well as the outlined shapes of ornate Buddhist temples make a pleasing, picture postcard scene. However, it isn't always easy to appreciate the surrounding beauty when fingers and toes are numb with cold! Accustomed to heat at the flick of a switch, the Stevenson family found the practice of inserting a coal brick under their clay floor had a few unwelcome drawbacks. Known as 'Ondo' the underground heating system may have enjoyed a reputation as an effective and affordable choice for inner city dwellers but there was a vast difference between suburbia's water heated pipes that ran neatly and unobtrusively through every room and its rural equivalent. Those living in poorer, isolated regions had to rely on compacted bricks that, once ignited, often released toxic and dangerous fumes. Reports of poisoning or even fatalities caused by inhaling the toxic vapours occurred with monotonous regularity. At one point, Billy and his family also succumbed to an overwhelming desire to drift into a nauseating but treacherous sleep. Only the intervention of a neighbour roused the little group from slumber and saved them from certain death.

Gradually, Billy's ministry spread to include American soldiers stationed at local army barracks as well as the inmates of Korean prisons. His previous experience of military life not mention his adventures into the world of criminal activity, provided a sense of empathy with both groups. Whether soldier or criminal, each man learned about God's pardon, mercy and love from the testimony of their Irish visitor. The former Shankill Road man had rarely preached to such an attentive and appreciative audience. However, it was his trips to the inhabitants of Korea's Sorok Island that proved an unforgettable and heart wrenching experience.

Situated less than a mile from the South Western port of Nokdong, the Island's landing stage warned visitor's of the dangers that waited. With bold letters a wooden placard announced that trespassers were likely to confront those whom society rejected and feared. Originally founded by the Japanese in 1910, Sorok Island was used as a containment centre for thousands of Koreans who suffered the trauma of Leprosy. The creation of a hospital on the site did little to alleviate sufferers' distress. In fact, the busiest department in the medical establishment was an operating theatre where thousands of individuals were robbed of limbs while involuntary sterilisations ensured they were also denied the potential joy of parenthood. By 1945, the island may have passed into the hands of Korean authorities but, instead of compassion, residents continued to endure a regime that was often described as callous and brutal.

Thirty-two years later, the placard of doom was replaced by a message of hope when modern education dispelled much of the myth and superstition that surrounded the disease. A notice announcing that 'leprosy is curable' endeavoured to reassure both visitors and victims. Within three decades, the construction of a bridge between Sorok and the mainland would provide islanders with a link to the outside world. But, in 1975, the people of Sorok continued to live an enforced and lonely existence. It was to this wounded element of suffering humanity that Billy Stevenson brought the message of God's love and salvation. At every opportunity, he boarded a boat and sailed across a thousand yards of sea to tell the colony of lepers how much Jesus loved them. No doubt Biblical accounts of the Lord's compassion and gentleness toward fellow sufferers touched a raw nerve of emotion among his Sorok listeners.

While her husband preached, Mary spent her time caring for their children. She may not have been able to do much about their basic living conditions but within a few months she had made some welcome additions to the family menu. Billy's favourite was a hot and spicy vegetable curry while his son and daughter preferred their mum's recipe for sponge cakes. Such treats may not have been as frequent as those at home but they were every bit as tasty. In Belfast, Mr Leckie's suggestion that Mary learn to cook may have seemed little more than an amusing and pleasant pastime but, in Korea, the skill proved invaluable. Many times Mary and Billy had cause to reflect on the providence of God in even the smallest detail.

Very often, Mary's 'wee buns' were appreciated as much by the local kids as by young Billy and Isabelle. Ingredients may not always have been freely available but when Mary had horded sufficient amounts of butter, sugar and flour and neighbours contributed a few eggs, the tiny cakes made an irresistible enticement to Mary's Bible classes. Going to the foot of the mountain, she would call to Harabudji, signalling that lessons were about to begin and it was time to round up the children. However, regardless of her love of the Korean people and their children, Mary continued to wrestle with severe and protracted bouts of homesickness. She missed her family and friends as well as the familiarity of her Northern Irish culture. The knowledge that God had led them to Asia offered reassurance and comfort but it didn't always ease the hurt. Her Korean neighbours did their best to make her feel welcome but Mary pined for a real sense of belonging.

Nine months after their arrival in Korea as she prepared to welcome the weekly bunch of chattering youngsters, Harabudji arrived with an urgent request. Excitedly and with no time for explanations, he insisted that Mary and Billy follow him. As they scrambled after their friend, the couple wondered what could have caused such a commotion. Breathless and confused they followed him through city streets and alleyways until finally, he turned and beckoning to Mary, pointed to the cause of his agitation and concern. Slowly, Mary stepped forward. At first, the tiny bundle appeared to be nothing more than a parcel of threadbare rags but as she moved closer, Mary caught a glimpse of a tiny fist waving shyly at the world. With her breath caught in her throat, the Belfast woman inched nearer and looked at the shock of silky black hair that peeked in little tufts above the thin cotton blanket. Gasping, she took the tiny infant in her arms, cradling her against the chill of Korea's winter winds. Billy, encircling his wife and the child in a tender embrace, added his own bodily protection against the icy blasts. A little note pinned to the makeshift blanket revealed the child's name, while the presence of an umbilical cord proclaimed her age. Less than an hour after she had entered the world, baby Kyung Sook Kim had been placed on a cold city pavement and left to die. Cocooned by innocence, the little scrap of humanity was unaware that the politics of poverty had decreed her death. For the first time in her short life she experienced the warmth of human tenderness and, snuggling against Mary's body, she drifted into a contented sleep. Gazing at the sleeping child, husband and wife were overwhelmed with compassion. It seemed incomprehensible that an innocent life should be so callously tossed aside. However, concern for the infant's welfare left no time for speculation on the subject and, hailing a taxi, they took the little girl to the nearest hospital.

For Mary and Billy, the discovery of an abandoned baby was an isolated and shocking incident. Yet, when they arrived at the hospital, they were distressed to learn that Kyung Sook Kim was just one of twenty-two infants who had been found that week. They listened in amazement as medical staff explained that due to food shortages, most of the children would not survive. There simply wasn't enough milk to go round. It was with a heavy heart that Mary and Billy left Kyung Sook Kim in the hospital's care. Returning home, the couple could not forget the Korean child that, for a brief while, had enjoyed the warmth of Mary's arms. As the night wore on, it became clear that Kyung Sook Kim had made a lasting impression on Mary Stevenson. Her newborn helplessness and vulnerability had stirred the maternal embers of Mary's heart. For the young missionary, motherhood was one of God's greatest blessings and her children, William junior and Isabelle her greatest treasures. Neither had Mary forgotten the children that she had carried for nine months only to lose at birth. There was no doubt that Mary had enough love to offer the Korean orphan, she just wasn't sure if they had enough food.

The proceeds from the sale of their Glengormley home had ensured that they did not impose a financial burden on their fellowship. Nevertheless, money does not have an elastic quality and the Stevenson family rapidly felt the pinch of hardship. However, Billy was adamant that they tell no-one of their situation. Instead he and Mary brought all their requests to God and trusted Him for protection and care. Unable to sleep, the couple talked long into the night. Billy knew that his wife longed to mother the Korean orphan. He too was moved by her plight but their family budget was already stretched to the limit. The last thing they needed was another mouth to feed. Yet, both Billy and

Mary had learned never to allow circumstances to cloud their judgement. Getting down on their knees, they asked God to guide them through the situation that would impact, not only their lives, but that of their children as well as little Kyung Sook Kim. By morning, husband and wife were on their way to collect their new daughter! Rushing into the hospital ward, Mary picked up the fragile bundle and held her close. Smiling, she whispered the words that, to outsiders may sound totally incoherent but between mother and child, is the language of love. To her first mother, the abandoned child would be remembered as Kyung Sook Kim but to the woman who would cherish and care for her, she would be known simply as Naomi, 'my delight.'

A new chapter had begun in the life of Mary and Billy as they left the hospital cradling the latest addition to the Stevenson family. Like all parents of a new arrival they could barely suppress their happiness as they took Naomi home to meet her brother and sister. Neither husband nor wife knew the depths of sorrow or the pinnacles of grace that lay ahead.

Chapter 11
FAMILY LIFE

LIKE ALL new babies, Naomi Stevenson's arrival met with a mixed reception. Excited at the prospect of a little sister, Isabelle and William showered her with a constant stream of kisses and hugs. Eagerly they scurried around helping Mary bathe, feed and tend their Korean sibling. Yet, blending families is never an easy or seamless process! Very often the ragged edges of uncertainty or childhood jealousy appear to mark the event. Uprooted from Western society Isabelle and William junior had been catapulted into a culture that at times seemed both alien and frightening. Separated from the valuable network of loving grandparents, aunts, uncles and cousins, they relied on their parents and each other for company and affection. As well as being brother and sister, Isabelle and William became best friends. The adoption of a Korean orphan, while an exciting and novel event, also meant having to share their parent's love which, for any child, is never easy. Most youngsters have nine months to prepare for a new baby in the home but for William and Isabelle, the family dynamics changed overnight.

Mary and Billy did their best to reassure their children that loving Naomi did not mean they loved them less. The constant affirmation of affection, plus the little girl's innocent charm, gradually won the heart of the Stevenson children. Before long, the brother and sister were among Naomi's greatest admirers! Billy and his wife may have been prepared for any childish expressions of resentment or envy but they did not anticipate the overt hostility they encountered from both sides of the community. While, many offered words of encouragement and support, there were those who ridiculed their decision to adopt a 'foreigner.' No doubt, much of the well meaning advice was prompted by genuine concern. Friends and family feared that the couple had allowed emotion to overrule logic and, at a future date, their actions would result in an identity crisis for Naomi and heartache for Mary and Billy. Nevertheless, the couple remained convinced that God had placed Naomi in their care. Ignoring the criticisms, they went ahead with their plan to legalise the adoption and left the details to God. Yet, it was impossible to prevent the occasional missive penetrating that sensitive and painful zone of the maternal heart. In public Mary's expression remained calm and composed but, in private, the tears flowed. As the weeks turned into months, life in the Stevenson home settled into a routine of Bible study, gospel meetings and preparing endless bottles of baby formulae. Unlike other infants, Naomi rarely interrupted her parent's sleep. In fact, compared to Mary's experience with William and Isabelle, her Korean daughter made very little fuss. The little girl slept or lay quietly, placidly accepting attention and care from her doting Irish family.

When Derick Bingham, accompanied by John Anderson and Bob Hewitt, held a gospel crusade in a South Korean sport's stadium during the summer of 1975, they had the privilege of witnessing over two hundred people place their trust in Christ. Among the numbers was a fifteen year old girl who was to make a huge impact on the Stevenson family. As a teenager Chung Sook provided her mother with a major source of income. Early each morning she left her home armed with a pile of newspapers that she spent the day trying to sell. Chung Sook's only desire was that, by the time the sun had traded places with the moon, all her papers would be sold and she could return home to an exhausted sleep. Failure to secure enough customers signalled a long and lonely night for the young woman.

Derick Bingham's message of God's love and salvation spoke directly to the girl's heart and with immense joy and gratitude she accepted Christ as her Saviour. Eager to begin her new life among those who loved the Lord, Chung Sook arrived at the local fellowship expecting nothing but the company of like minded believers. Instead she found a whole new way of life. For many Koreans, embracing the Christian faith often resulted in exclusion from friends and family while a few met with much more tragic circumstances. Mary and Billy were among those who listened with shock and despair at the news of a young Korean sister who, because of her faith in Christ, had been set alight and burned by an outraged husband. The woman lived but for the rest of her life she bore the painful and public reminder that she belonged to the Lord.

Chung Sook's presence in their gathering was a source of concern as well as delight. Understanding her plight, the elders realised that she needed physical as well as spiritual nurture. They also knew that one of their young brothers and his wife could do with some practical help in their home. Chung Sook and the Stevenson family seemed an ideal match! Politely and with great respect, they asked their Korean sister if she would like to live with the 'foreigners' and, in return for her help, they would supply food and lodging. At the same time Billy was also approached and asked if he could accommodate their request. By this stage in their service, Billy and Mary had run out of even the most basic essentials. Food was in short supply and very often mealtimes began and ended with Billy's word of thanksgiving. Leaving the table with an empty stomach never seemed to bother the Irish man but Mary often found it difficult to wait for God's provision. Nevertheless, He never failed and on many occasions, the couple would open their door to find neighbours and friends had left a basket of fresh eggs and groceries. After listening to the suggestion regarding Chung Sook, Billy and Mary agreed to accept the girl into their home. Carefully, the Shankill Road man explained his terms. When they had food, Chung Sook would eat. If they had money, she would have her share but when they had nothing, the Korean girl would partake of their need. With excitement and gratitude she accepted the simple conditions and moved into her new home. Few realised the blessing that Chung Sook would bring to the Stevenson family.

Quickly Chung Sook adapted to the new routine. She helped with the household chores, looked after Naomi while Mary visited the sick and elderly and played a major role in the children's Bible classes. With the aid of Chung Sook's interpretation skills combined with Mary's considerable miming ability, the lessons developed a lively and fun filled atmosphere. Local children flocked to hear the 'foreign' woman's stories about a man called Jesus. Mary and Chung Sook rapidly developed a friendship that was to span both continents and decades.

Finally, Mary's heart had settled and her homesickness eased. William and Isabelle had adapted to their new environment, Billy was preaching constantly, her Bible classes were proving a popular and successful venue while Chung Sook was a constant source of blessing and inspiration. However, it was in the face of her little adopted daughter that Mary read the true purpose of her presence in Asia. Naomi, with her Korean heritage provided a tangible link to the people they had come to serve. In her tiny features, Mary also saw the innocent vulnerability that tugs so fiercely at every mother's heartstrings. With the satisfaction of maternal nurture, God had sated her craving for the familiar surroundings of her Irish home.

While Chung Sook and Mary shared many happy moments, as well as a lot of laughter, there was nothing the Belfast woman and her husband loved more than news of Ireland. Derick Bingham's stay in Korea proved a perfect opportunity for the friends to indulge in a quick trip down memory lane. During a visit to the Stevenson's home, he shared a time of fellowship as well as a cup of tea. No doubt they compared the terrible taste of Harabudji's boiled orange peel to its preferable and more digestible 'Tetley' equivalent. As the evening wore on they talked with fond remembrance of gifted Ulster speakers whose ministry had made an impact on all their lives. Perhaps, they reminisced over gospel rallies where God had poured out His Spirit and saved many sinners. Whatever the content of their conversation, it was Derick's observation of their Korean daughter that sent a chill of fear through Mary's heart. Quietly and pensively the Northern Ireland author and preacher remarked that Naomi was, "frighteningly good." At five months, the black haired infant regarded the world with a solemn but impassive expression. Undoubtedly at the sight of Mary, Billy or one of her siblings, the little face would glow with the warmth of recognition and delight but, she demanded nothing. No whine of impatience or querulous fatigue. For a child so young, Naomi had an abundant supply of patience.

For William and Isabelle, Naomi's presence in the home caused less upset than expected. Yet, Isabelle never quite got over the concern that her mum would end up adopting the whole Korean nation! Mary's discovery of an orphanage on the outskirts of town only fuelled the child's suspicions. Every week, the Irish missionary set off on a four hour journey only to return with four or five Korean orphans in tow. After bathing, feeding and removing their head lice, she told them stories of Jesus and allowed them to spend the night in her daughter's room. The next day she would take them back to the orphanage only to repeat the process the following week. As far as Mary was concerned, she was merely providing the youngsters with an oasis of love in an otherwise bleak existence but for Isabelle, sharing her room with a handful of strangers wasn't always an enjoyable experience. It would take years for her to appreciate the huge reservoirs of love in her mother's heart.

While Billy and Mary's days were occupied in spreading the news of God's unfathomable mercy, their nights turned to thoughts of Naomi. Together, husband and wife knelt before the Throne of Grace and poured out their worries at the complexities of the Korean legal system. Neither Billy nor Mary had the skill to decipher the intricacies of adoption law. All they knew was that they had grown to love the child and did not want to lose her. In future years, they would recall those moments when loving Naomi was all that mattered.

Chapter 12
DAMAGED GOODS

IN 1975, Gerald Ford was steering the United States gently through the aftermath of the Watergate era. Thrust into an office he hadn't sought, the American President was perceived by many as a reassuring and reliable figure. Across the Atlantic, Northern Ireland was also emerging from a political crisis as Merlyn Rees, the Province's Secretary of State, released the remaining forty six people that had been held without trial during the period known as 'internment.' But politics wasn't the only topic dominating the headlines. In May of the same year, a tornado tore through the State of Nebraska claiming lives and devastating property. With over a billion dollars worth of insurance claims, the disaster was reckoned to one of the costliest in American history. Media attention shifted to South Korea when the disappearance of a local fisherman sparked claims that he had been abducted by neighbouring North Korea. Thirty-two years later the story would once again make the headlines when fifty-nine year old Lee Han-Seop escaped and was re-united with his wife and family in South Korea's capital city of Seoul. Unfortunately there are few unreservedly happy endings. Perhaps the fact that her husband had acquired another family during his time in the North detracted somewhat from the reunion.

However, regardless of what damage was inflicted on Northern Irish politics, Nebraska's population or relations between North and South Korea, for Mary and Billy Stevenson, 1975 had only one notable event. History might record the destructive force of nature's fury as well as the various sagas of political and human intrigue but, the private agony of the couple from Belfast would be known only to God. By the time she was ten months old, Naomi had become an integral part of the Stevenson family. The sight of the Irish foreigner with a Korean child at her hip was a familiar spectacle in the Seoul neighbourhood. Local children couldn't resist the studied gaze of the doll like infant who sat on Chung Sook's or Mrs Stevenson's knee during Bible class. Their mothers may have envied Mary the youngster's placid and even temperament but many breathed a sigh of relief at the boisterous, though exhaustive inquisitiveness of their own offspring. Yet, if any Korean mums wondered at Naomi's malleable impassiveness no-one voiced their concern. However, one of Mary's friends, an American missionary named Flo, did attempt to broach the subject. Gently she pointed out the similarity in age between her little boy Timmy and Mary's daughter Naomi. While young Timmy was trying out his sturdy little legs, Mary's child tended to flop on the floor and wait to be carried. Quietly, Flo suggested that such a difference in development might indicate an underlying medical problem. Understandably, Mary didn't want to acknowledge the truth of her friend's observations. Neither did she want to confront the fear that gnawed suspiciously at her heart.

Yet, Naomi's apparent lack of development continued to bother Flo and, as the date for their baby's vaccination shots drew closer, she invited Mary to bring the child to see her family paediatrician. With no money for food never mind polio jabs, Mary accepted her friend's suggestion with welcome relief. Once at the doctor's office, Flo discreetly expressed her concern at Naomi's rate of development and asked if the medical expert would mind examining the child extra closely. After inspecting Naomi, the doctor returned her to Mary's arms and confessed that he could find nothing wrong. In an attempt to address Flo's fears, he explained how, in his opinion, it was merely a question of nationality rather than any systemic dysfunction that was at the root of the problem. Assuring the women that Asian babies were inclined to develop at a slower rate than their Western cousins, he calmly ushered them out of his office. No doubt, Mary's relief at the diagnosis outweighed any sense of outrage at either the patronising tone or any implication of racism.

Mollified by the paediatrician's explanation, Mary and Billy buried their concern and looked forward to finalising the adoption. Eventually, after months of negotiating and endless bureaucracy, the trio arrived at the agent's office, eager to complete the formalities. Naomi had already taken up residence in the Stevenson's affections and, within a few moments would become a fully fledged and legal member of their family. For Mary and Billy the last moments in the process proved the most trying. At any second, their daughter's biological parents could have a change of heart and decide they wanted to keep her. Nothing was certain until the Korean authorities had officially released her into their care. Shortly after their arrival, a Korean nurse entered the room and took Naomi to be photographed and examined by the agency's doctor. Less than five minutes later she returned and the meeting came to an abrupt end. There was nothing for Mary and Billy to do but return home and await the outcome.

The Stevenson family had endured many anxious times since arriving in Korea but waiting for the adoption representative to call was among the most nerve wrecking. At every step in their journey they had sought God's guidance. Both Mary and Billy knew they could depend on Him to resolve the situation regarding Naomi. Nevertheless, the heart is a tender area and the couple realised the incredible pain that waited if they were to be denied their Korean daughter. Once again they brought their pleas to the Throne of Grace and pouring out their fears and desires made their petitions known to God.

Finally the shrill cry of the phone rent the air. Regarding each other, Mary and Billy hesitated, reading the hope as well as the fear in each others eyes. Picking up the receiver, they heard the verdict they had dreaded. It was not possible to adopt Naomi. Immediately, their thoughts spun to the little girl's natural parents. Had mercy finally melted their heart? Had they discovered a way to provide for her welfare? Crushed beneath the weight of losing their dark eyed child, tears blinded their eyes. Slowly as they listened, comprehension began to dawn. Naomi's parents had not had second thoughts. There was no loving family waiting to claim her. With calm and precise deliberation, the adoption representative outlined the reason why they could not have her. According to their medical expert, the child suffered from Cerebral Palsy and had been labelled 'damaged goods.'

The medical prognosis promised Naomi a bleak and frightening future. Her damaged brain, unable to co-ordinate the thin and unresponsive limbs would eventually confine her to life in a wheel chair. For Naomi the passing of the years would bring neither the joys of first love nor its heartache. She would never know the excitement of the school prom, the satisfaction of success or even the luxury of a best friend. The exquisite happiness of a bridal walk and the consuming love of motherhood were destined for other girls but not the Korean orphan. Regardless of her surroundings or chronological age, Naomi would live in a perpetual world of childlike innocence.

Devastated by the extent of the child's problem, Mary and Billy struggled to comprehend the severity of the diagnosis as well as its future implications. Hoping for guidance and information, they turned to the adoption agency but were staggered by the response. Instead of support and reassurance the official calmly offered an alternative solution to their 'problem.' Viewed as 'damaged' Naomi was no longer a candidate for adoption and would be immediately withdrawn. In her place, the couple would be provided with another healthy and more suitable baby. Astonished, Mary and Billy felt as though they were at the customer services department in one of Belfast's High Street Stores. But instead of a skirt or a sweater they were talking about rejecting a human life.

Whatever else was on the menu that evening, the Stevenson home was awash with tears. Concerned for the child but hurt by such an overt display of human callousness, Mary wept for the Korean child. Encircled in Billy's arms, she buried her head against his shoulder and sobbed out her pain. No doubt memories of two other infants who had been denied the opportunity of life came flooding back as husband and wife surrendered to grief. Yet, before the evening ended, Mary and Billy had once again found a balm for their pain. In the presence of God, they waited as His peace and grace flowed through hearts and minds, restoring, and comforting, bringing strength for the days ahead.

Lying together in the stillness of the Korean night, husband and wife whispered softly. There was no doubt in their mind. God had led them, not only to Korea but to the pitiful bundle that lay like a discarded parcel on a city street. It didn't matter that her body was broken and her mind locked in permanent childhood, Mary and Billy's love was unconditional. Whatever the future held, they would commit their path to God. Surprised by their decision, the Korean authorities proceeded to finalise the adoption and before long Naomi was an official member of the Stevenson family. Few could have guessed how the child whom the world had labelled 'damaged goods' would prove a blessing at home as well as abroad.

Chapter 13
THE HERO

WITHIN A year of their arrival in Seoul, Mary and Billy had won the respect and affection of their Korean neighbours. Their home rapidly became the first port of call when illness or trouble struck the little community. With a blend of sympathetic concern and down to earth pragmatism, the couple managed to find solutions to most of life's minor catastrophes. Cajoling and encouraging, they soothed the pains and anxieties that poverty and desperation indiscriminately inflict.

However, the unrelenting stream of visitors plus the demands of a new baby rapidly began to take its toll. The painful shock of Naomi's diagnosis may have settled to a dull ache but caring for the tiny infant was often sheer hard work. Before long Mary and Billy were completely exhausted. Yet, it wasn't only husband and wife who felt the strain. Their children also experienced the bewilderment and stress of having to share mum and dad with most of the neighbourhood. Naomi's presence, while a blessing to the infant as well as her adoptive parents was initially a source of childish annoyance for ten year old Isabelle. For Mary and Billy the constant round of appointments with doctors and therapists was undoubtedly a labour of love but for their young daughter, it often seemed more like an unwelcome endurance test. Every week, the little girl accompanied her mum and adopted sister in the search for medical expertise. Belfast's transport system may have had its faults but, compared to the over crowded and stifling heat of its Asian equivalent, the city's bus service was nothing short of luxurious. Throughout her adult life Isabelle would associate the heady aroma of exotic spices mixed with the overpowering stench of body odour, as a necessary but dreaded part of her childhood experiences. As well as disrupting her daily routine, the little girl quickly discovered that the Korean infant evoked a whole new range of emotions. Like many siblings of special needs children, Isabelle encountered an unfamiliar sense of jealous resentment. To ten year old logic, the fact that Naomi was abandoned at birth seemed to confer some kind of priority status with the adult world. Her medical complications only served to heighten her value making her 'extra special.' In an attempt to impress their children with Naomi's vulnerability and need, Mary and Billy had inadvertently made her an object of envy. Isabelle, hoping for an extra dose of attention occasionally wished that she too was 'special.'

Nevertheless, regardless of the intermittent bouts of jealousy, Isabelle never doubted that her parents loved her. During his unsaved days, Billy may have caused his children many anxious and embarrassing moments but from the moment he accepted Christ as his Saviour, Billy became unrecognisable. Mary not only got a new husband, the children received a better and different father. As far as Isabelle Stevenson was concerned, her dad was her hero.

As with all such champions, Billy was called to star in some dramatic rescues! The first occurred after his daughter decided to explore the nearby Buddhist temple. Accompanied by Chung Sook she clambered along the mountain's foothills until she reached the temple's courtyard. The climb proved hard work and the child quickly developed a raging thirst. At first glance, the little font of water she found seemed to be just what she needed. Without thinking, Isabelle cupped her hands and greedily drank the foul tasting liquid. Instead of a mountain spring, the youngster had gulped what the Monks considered to be holy water. Little wonder that, after months of stagnating in a shallow receptacle, the water should be laced with a variety of nasty bacteria and before long Isabelle began to experience some frightening symptoms. Her head and legs ached while her temperature soared as she stumbled and tripped her way back home. Running ahead, Chung Sook managed to raise the alarm but, by the time Isabelle fell through the front door and into Mary's arms, it was obvious that the child was desperately ill. Frantically Mary tried to lower the little girl's fever with cold compresses but it was obvious the child needed urgent medical attention. Yet, with a strictly enforced curfew that brooked no excuses, Billy and Mary realised the danger of leaving the house after dark. However, parental love is a much stronger force than any government policy. Slipping out, Billy quietly and with great stealth made his way through deserted and eerie streets to obtain the necessary doctor's permission that would allow them to take Isabelle to hospital. Within a few hours, doctors had confirmed that Isabelle was suffering from a severe case of meningitis and as he sat by his daughter's bedside, Billy Stevenson realised how close he had come to losing his beloved child. With an overwhelming sense of gratitude, he offered a prayer of thanksgiving.

Her dad's determination to find help despite the threat of danger as well as his bedside vigil is among some of Isabelle's fondest memories. Yet, Billy's heroic quality, not to mention swimming prowess, was once again put to the test! Worn down by months of fatigue, the couple was persuaded to bring the family and spend a few hours relaxing in the company of other missionaries at one of Asia's glistening white beaches. Surrounded by scenery whose beauty lulled and absorbed the senses, Mary and Billy slowly began to unwind. Their eyes took in the splendour of God's handiwork while their nostrils feasted on the fresh, spray filled air that blows from the Yellow Sea. As well as contributing to the atmospheric pleasantries, the Yellow Sea is known for its dangerous tides and currents. During August, the monsoon season adds dramatically to the volume of water, making the area particularly treacherous. In an effort to warn the public and avoid tragedy, Korean authorities implemented a 'red flag' system. Strung across the deceptive waters, a series of crimson poles urged caution and forbade anyone to swim.

However, to Isabelle and her young Korean friend, the excitement of climbing aboard a rubber ring and paddling out into the water proved irresistible. Initially the youngsters giggled with delight as they bobbed about on the gentle waves that lapped gently near the shore. But, laughter turned to screams of terror when their makeshift craft was caught in an underwater current and began swirling further from land and toward the open sea. Within moments, the girls were no longer able to see the sea bed and, despite their youth, realised that they were completely out of their depth. Fear and panic began to set in as Isabelle scanned the shoreline, desperate for a glimpse of her dad. Like little dots, people walked along the beach oblivious to the youngsters' dilemma. With only a rubber ring to keep them afloat, Isabelle and her friend knew it was only a matter of time before the angry waves tossed them to their death. Terrified they clung to the flimsy float and screamed for help. Just when it seemed that things couldn't get much worse, an enormous swell dashed them against one of the numerous rocks that rose treacherously from the sea bed. Cut and bleeding, the sobbing children held on to their rapidly deflating raft. At her wits end, Isabelle looked up at the mountain that ran along one side of the shore only to fall away in a rocky precipice far out to sea. To her amazement, she saw a familiar figure outlined against the afternoon sky. Squinting against the rays of the strong sunlight, Isabelle felt a quiver of excitement race through her. There was no mistake, the man walking along, engaged in deep conversation with his friend, was her dad! Screaming at the top of her voice, the little girl shouted for help. Instinctively she knew that her dad would rescue them.

As soon as Billy caught sight of the children bobbing on the water below, he understood the urgency of their plight. Already punctured by the constant dashing against the rocks, their little ring would soon disintegrate, leaving the helpless kids at the mercy of the Yellow Sea. Without explanation he ran toward the edge of the rocks, leaving his companion startled at the sudden burst of activity. Slipping and sliding, he stumbled and fell toward the deep and dangerous water. Aware that the children's panic could drown them all he measured his tone. With calm and soothing words he reassured his daughter that her dad still had the magic touch! He would save them both but he needed Isabelle to demonstrate confidence and trust. Depending on his daughter's response, the Korean child would either relax, allowing him to bring them safely to shore or continue to fight with blind terror and take them all to a watery grave. At one time, trusting the man who drove them at break neck speed into gangland danger would have seemed laughable but Isabelle had witnessed the power of salvation in her father's life. She knew the gentleness that flows from a paternal heart. Without hesitation, she smiled her understanding and entered into Billy's childlike game of rescuing damsels in distress. Over two hours later, the threesome clambered onto the relative safety of the rocks. Bruised, battered and bleeding, they lay exhausted, thankful to be alive. Running to gather her daughter into her arms, Mary was enveloped by feelings of relief and joy. There was no doubt in Isabelle's young heart that she was indeed a very precious and 'special' child. God had brought her dad five thousand miles to South Korea in order to rescue the lost but He had also placed him on a rocky outcrop overlooking the Yellow Sea, not only to save his little girl's life but carve a tender place in her heart.

Surrounded by a happy crowd of well wishers, Billy Stevenson was the hero of the day. Yet, no doubt, the man who appreciated Billy as well as owed him most was the companion who had walked with him along the rocky pathway. Billy had saved two children that afternoon. One was his daughter Isabelle the other was the Korean man's little girl who took her cue from the Irish child and trusted her life to Billy Stevenson.

Chapter 14
HEALTH ISSUES

IN SEOUL, apart from an iron clad stomach, shopping for groceries didn't normally require any additional protection. Within six months, Mary had grown accustomed to the Korean cuisine and the sight of dog chops and steaks, although distasteful, failed to send her into a cultural frenzy! However, an armour plated helmet might have spared the young mother many months of disorientating vertigo. The incident that knocked Mary's balance into a spinning orbit occurred when a heavy metal sign fell from a local shop and hit her on the head. Concussed and lying prostrate on the ground, Mary had no idea that life was about to adopt a permanent tilt. The next time she opened her eyes the world had shifted out of focus and was to remain that way for almost two years. Hugging the pavement, the Irish missionary tried desperately to re-gain control of her senses but every time she tried to stand, the world literally moved.

Rushed to hospital, Mary underwent an immediate barrage of tests yet, no-one seemed able to find a solution to her problem. The best that the Korean doctors could offer was a daily bowl of seaweed soup which did nothing for her dizziness and only added to the nausea. It was during those depressing and, at times, frightening days that the Stevenson family began to appreciate the full blessing of Chung Sook's presence in their home. Unable to stand without falling over, Mary sat on the floor of her home and did her best to preside over the business of daily life. William junior and Isabelle were old enough to fend for themselves but Naomi was a constant source of worry. Helpless and vulnerable, the child depended on her mum for everything. Billy did his best to lend a hand but it was obvious that the family needed some additional support. When Chung Sook stepped in and assumed responsibility for the little girl's care, no-one could have been better suited to the task. Already a familiar face in the Stevenson home, the Korean teenager was well used to Naomi's routine. In turn the baby recognised and trusted her young carer and was spared any anxious moments that a stranger may have brought to her tiny world. Relieved of the physical burden of looking after her family, Mary thanked God for once again meeting their need with such perfect provision and wisdom.

As the weeks progressed, the awful sensation of disorientation had settled to an uncomfortable, though manageable, feeling of light headedness. Instead of spinning out of control, Mary found that she was able to stagger her way through the day. Yet, while the level of Mary's health problems dropped from acute to chronic; Billy's life was suddenly and dramatically hanging in the balance. Initially, the aches and pains seemed little more than an annual bout of flu but when his normally healthy complexion took on a greyish hue, Mary insisted her husband go straight to bed. Shivering beneath the covers, Billy wondered what was wrong. He'd had several attacks of influenza over the years but nothing compared to the deathly pallor or searing pains of his current illness. But it wasn't until he opened his eyes to see John Anderson and another brother from the local fellowship, on their knees at his bedside that Billy began to suspect he was suffering from more than a seasonal chill. Several visitors had already noticed the Shankill Road man's unusual lack of energy and realised something was seriously wrong. For weeks the couple's Christian friends had made their ailing brother the subject of many prayers but Billy's condition appeared to go from bad to worse.

On one occasion, desperate to use the bathroom, he waited until everyone had left the room before grabbing the opportunity for a few moments privacy. Climbing out of bed he made his way unsteadily across the room and into the hallway but, just as he reached the tiny closet, his body revealed its mutinous intentions and unleashed a huge jettison of crimson blood. As the life sustaining liquid poured from every orifice, splashing both floor and walls, Billy stumbled and fell back toward the bedroom. The sight of the bloody mess provoked both mortal fear and anaemic shock. Yet, the emotion uppermost in his mind was embarrassment. Like many of his generation, Billy felt a sense of shame at any loss of bodily control. The prospect of his family or friends viewing his soiled and stained pyjamas was a situation to be avoided at all costs. Ignoring the rapidly approaching blackness that threatened to swallow the last remnants of consciousness, he locked the door, determined to clean the room before his guests returned.

Noticing the trail of blood, Chung Sook ran to raise the alarm. Panicked and distraught, Mary, accompanied by Wilbur Kirk and Wesley Barr from Northern Ireland, ran to Billy's room. Eventually, with a combination of emotional pleading and desperation, they managed to persuade him to open the door. At the sight of her husband's ashen and semi-conscious appearance, Mary realised just how urgent the situation had become. Distraught at the very real possibility she might lose the man she loved, Mary cradled the pathetic figure in her arms, determined to infuse him with a little of her of own spiritual and physical strength. Adding a protective layer of warmth, their friend Wesley Barr used his coat to wrap Billy against the deathly chill of bodily shock, and, between them, they carried him to the visitor's borrowed car.

Billy may have struggled to retain consciousness throughout the ordeal but by the time they reached the local emergency department, he willingly and gratefully surrendered to the comforting folds of dark oblivion. Unsure as to the exact nature of his problem, doctors decided that the best course of action was to carry out an endoscophy procedure. Thirty years later, the practice of slipping a slim, flexible tube into a patient's stomach would be done with the minimum of fuss or discomfort but, in the mid seventies, its South Korean predecessor was neither easy nor pleasant. While Mary and a couple of their friends pinned the terrified man to the table, a doctor proceeded to insert, what Billy believed to be the rough end of a brush shaft, into his throat. Choking and gagging he swallowed the implement and within a few minutes the professional gave his diagnosis. Billy was suffering from a perforated duodenal ulcer. With such rapidly depleting haemoglobin levels, his condition was critical. Unless he received an immediate blood transfusion, there was nothing the medical experts could do.

As far as Mary was concerned, the medical jargon was every bit as foreign as the Korean language. X-ray results, endoscope reports and haemoglobin counts were technical terms that meant nothing to the perplexed and frightened woman. Nevertheless, it didn't take a degree in either language or medicine to understand the meaning behind the doctor's grave expression. Unless they stabilise her husband's condition and start treatment immediately, Billy would die. With no funds at their disposal, Mary knew she could not pay for essential blood transfusions never mind any additional therapy. However, their Christian journey, especially their experiences in South Korea had taught many valuable lessons. Mary Stevenson knew the power of prayer. She had witnessed God's amazing provision when food was scant and money scarce. The tiny Belfast woman had basked in the warmth of God's love and faithfulness on many occasions and believed He would help them now. She had no idea what she could trade for the priceless currency of donated blood. Yet, it didn't matter. Her Father in Heaven would undertake. Once again, as she had done on numerous occasions in the past, Mary brought their need to the Throne of Grace and waited for Him to provide.

The answer was as swift as it was miraculous. The months of love, patience and kindness invested in their South Korean community reaped an unexpected reward. The next time she arrived at the hospital's entrance, the devoted wife gazed in astonishment at the sight that met her eyes. Waiting quietly in a line that reached far beyond the doors and into Seoul's busy streets, was the answer to her prayers. Without hesitation, the South Korean people, having heard of Billy's plight, came to offer the ultimate and precious gift of blood.

Billy and Mary Stevenson had arrived among them armed with nothing but patience and kindness. They had shared in their poverty, laughed at the drama as well as the absurdities of life and, when heartache intruded, partook of their sorrow. They had met them on an equal footing with neither expectations nor demands. Their home like their hearts was perpetually open as they demonstrated the true nature of Christian love. In the faces of the people who waited to save her husband's life, Mary read, not only a measure of their family's acceptance in Seoul, but a wonderful illustration of God's grace and providential care. Within a few hours, Billy's condition was declared stable. The donations of blood proved more than adequate and nurses were sent to dismiss the crowd that continued to wait. However, as Mary made her way home that evening she had another prescription for God to fill. Having provided many pints of blood, five tickets to Belfast International Airport shouldn't pose a problem!

Chapter 15
THE HOMECOMING
☙

BILLY'S ENCOUNTER with South Korea's medical experts undoubtedly saved his life. Staunching the flow of blood, doctors stabilised his condition and enabled him to return to Belfast for further treatment and immediate surgery. Throughout their time in Seoul, the family received many tokens of kindness when neighbours and members of their fellowship brought fresh eggs, a few groceries and milk for baby Naomi. Yet, there was no gift as valuable or as much appreciated as the generous donation of blood. Both Mary and Billy were acutely aware of the depth of gratitude they owed.

An operation was a difficult prescription but a diet of rice water was even harder to swallow. The thin, insipid liquid did nothing to sate either Billy's hunger or tempt his taste buds. Nevertheless, Mary was determined that her husband adhere to the bland regime. As the days passed, Billy often regretted that James Leckie had ever suggested Mary learn to cook. Her ability to rustle up a spicy dish of curried vegetables from even the most basic ingredients had often been a source of welcome admiration but, as the tempting odours wafted through the house, Billy found his wife's talent an exquisite form of torture!

Over the coming weeks, the Stevenson family had yet another reason to thank God for Mr Leckie's generosity. Throughout their friendship the wealthy businessman had demonstrated the more practical nature of brotherly love. As well as spiritual guidance, he had poured in the soothing oils of support and encouragement. Neither had he withheld the precious commodity of time. With patience, he had accompanied Billy through long hours of darkness as he made his way slowly and painfully toward the light of salvation. Like the Good Samaritan of scripture, James Leckie did not baulk when it came to sharing his portion of worldly wealth. Whether it was a word in season, a comfortable chair or even the deposit for a home, the kindly benefactor contributed from his storehouse of earthly riches. Three years later, he once again proved God's instrument of blessing when he met the couple's need and paid their return fares to Belfast.

With the problem of finance settled, Mary and Billy heaved a sigh of relief. Yet it wasn't long before another obstacle was occupying their mind and prayers. Without a passport, Naomi would not be able to leave South Korea. Once again, another Christian man took up their cause. Acting on their behalf, their friend Stu Mitchell cut a path through the maze of South Korean bureaucracy and managed to secure the necessary documentation that would enable Naomi to meet her Northern Irish relatives. Boarding the huge aircraft, the family's thoughts were already soaring toward the streets of Belfast. Each with their individual memories looked forward with a mixture of excitement and apprehension. Billy, although eager to share the news of God's work in Seoul, did not relish the prospect of an operation. Mary, bursting with happiness at the prospect of a family reunion, dreaded confronting her father's illness. While their mother and father dreamed of re-newing acquaintances, William junior and his sister Isabelle knew that their world had already disappeared. Three years may be a short gap in the adult realm but for children it is the equivalent of a lifetime.

Just as Mary and Billy dreamed of meeting with loved ones, their family and friends also counted the moments to the arrival of the British Airway's connecting flight from Hong Kong. However, both were due for a bitter disappointment. Technical problems with the aircraft necessitated a three day stop over on the beautiful island. Despite their initial frustration, the family's spirits soon perked up at the realisation they were to be accommodated in one of the city's most prestigious hotels. Best of all, the airline had agreed to pay all expenses! Bedrooms with ensuite facilities not to mention soft, fluffy white towels were a luxury the family had never experienced. Yet, when they arrived at the establishment's restaurant, the foursome could barely believe their eyes! Trays of smoked salmon, roast beef, cured ham and tender chicken breast were laid out in a tempting array that had their mouths watering with anticipation. Almost fainting with hunger and deprived of the sensation of taste, Billy reached for a spicy morsel. Just when the savoury paradise was within his grasp, Mary intervened and snatched it away. Throughout their marriage, Billy had begged his wife for many things including forgiveness, but a slice of spicy meat had never been one of them! For the remainder of their stay, Billy spooned his watery diet while Mary and the children feasted on Hong Kong's exotic cuisine.

The Ulster Worker's Council strike of 1974 that brought the Province to a standstill had ended. But within three years Northern Ireland was once again facing the threat of widespread industrial action. The underlying issues may have changed but the consequences of the United Unionist Action Council's political protest heralded yet another helping of chaos and economic instability. As far as Billy Stevenson and his family were concerned, Northern Ireland had altered little during their absence. However, while their troubled homeland remained the same, Mary and Billy Stevenson had been transformed. Just three years previously, the Belfast missionaries had boarded a plane and headed into an unknown future. Mary, clinging with white knuckled terror as the aircraft soared far into the clouds had wondered when or if she would see her family again. Yet, in 1977 as the plane descended with a bumpy thud, onto Aldergrove's rain splashed runway, there was no resemblance between the confident sun bronzed woman with a Korean baby strapped to her lap and the fearful woman she had once been. Mary and Bill, as missionaries, had been moulded and shaped as they experienced the day to day reality of God's amazing grace and providential care.

Their arrival in Belfast heralded many happy hours but ironically the reunion with loved ones also signalled the first separation between husband and wife. Unable to accommodate all five visitors, Mary and the children stayed with her family while, after many years, Billy once again moved in with his mum and dad.

As news of their arrival spread, the McMillan and Stevenson homes were inundated with visitors. Eager to hear of the Lord's work in South Korea and, concerned by reports of Billy's illness, friends from the surrounding assemblies, including their home fellowship at Fortwilliam Gospel Hall, called to see the couple, offering encouragement and prayer. Neighbours also flocked, curious to learn about the couple's missionary lifestyle but no doubt hoping for a glimpse of the tiny foreigner that now accompanied them. Thirty years later, the adoption of children from other cultures would become almost fashionable but in the mid seventies, Mary's South Korean daughter was an unusual sight. Everywhere she went the raven haired youngster with her olive complexion and almond shaped eyes became the focus of attention. Suddenly everyone wanted to know the story of how a Korean orphan had found her way into the Stevensons' hearts as well as their home. When Gloria Honeyford, a local television and radio presenter, invited Billy to share their experiences, he seized the opportunity to tell listeners of how God had changed their lives and, with infinite wisdom, led them five thousand miles to rescue a child from certain death. Slowly Mary and Billy began to realise that Naomi's presence in their family was more than a mutual blessing. Apart from her natural Oriental charm, the little girl painted a picture of mercy and grace. But neither of her adopted parents could have imagined just how close to home the divine illustration would reach.

Among the many visitors that called, the one Billy dreaded most was his doctor! The Christian surgeon from Belfast's Royal Victoria Hospital brought the inevitable confirmation that an operation was imminent. However, before surgery could proceed, Billy's physical condition needed improvement. There was only one way to gain the necessary strength. The Irish missionary had to eat! Amazed, the delighted patient queried the prescription, explaining how his South Korean doctors had insisted he take nothing but rice water. With a chuckle the surgeon agreed that, in the early days, immediately following his health crisis, that had been an excellent choice but once the initial threat had passed, he could and should have returned to a normal diet. When the doctor had gone, Billy remembered the beautiful Hong Kong hotel restaurant and the numerous trays of delectable delights that he had been denied. Perhaps, as he recalled Mary's adamant refusal to allow him to sample even a tiny morsel, their enforced separation was a blessing in disguise!

Chapter 16
THE FURLOUGH

AS AN ex military man Billy Stevenson knew all about the meaning of furlough. At one time, bored and disillusioned by the soldier's lot, he had sought every opportunity to secure the official leave of absence that would provide a few weeks of respite and peace. But as a Christian, even the hardships of the mission field did not tempt him to abdicate from the service of God. Bringing the gospel message to people who were lost had a satisfying and unique reward. The knowledge of lives changed and infused with hope was a precious experience that Billy constantly wanted to repeat. When illness eventually enforced a period of rest, Billy waited with impatient restraint for the moment he could return to South Korea.

Mary, like her husband missed their Korean brothers and sisters. She was also more than a little homesick for the company of Chung Sook whose inability to secure a passport had required her to remain in Seoul. Yet, Mary took comfort from the fact that the young woman wasn't too disappointed by her exclusion from the visit to Ireland. A budding romance with a handsome member of their South Korean fellowship ensured that Chung Sook's attention as well as her time was well occupied! Instead of fretting, Mary seized every opportunity to revel in the warmth of her family's company. Over numerous cups of tea, her parents and siblings listened as Mary regaled them with stories of life in another culture. Her hilarious accounts of how Korean cuisine had shocked their Western taste buds elicited sighs of sympathy as well as gales of laughter. But very often as Mary's reminiscences turned toward the market places of Seoul where children, dressed in rags, begged for food, it was sorrow and not mirth that provoked an avalanche of tears.

Whatever Mr and Mrs McMillan made of their daughter's adventures, they had nothing but admiration and respect for her willingness to adopt and love a child that was not her own. While most people in the Shankill Road community regarded Naomi with compassionate affection, Mary's mum and dad knew that the three year old child was not immune to the cruelty of racial intolerance. Already Mary and Billy had noticed that several invitations to informal social events were on the condition that Naomi did not accompany them. With great sadness Mr and Mrs McMillan realised that their daughter and son-in-law had embarked on a journey that, as well as joy, would always be fraught with pain. Whether it was the little girl's ancestral lineage or her profound disability, Naomi Stevenson would always attract attention. For now, the soft, pretty contours of infancy may lend a cushion against the harsher realities of life but as the marred imperfections of adulthood became increasingly noticeable, Mary and Billy would find themselves relegated to the periphery of society. Nevertheless, as she cooed and whispered to her Korean child, Mr and Mrs McMillan witnessed in their daughter's expression an emotion that went beyond natural affection. Enhanced by the firelight, they saw a quality of love that could surmount every obstacle. Imbued with the same maternal attributes, Mary's mother understood the strength of motherly bonds. Her daughter's obvious delight in the children she fondly and teasingly referred to as her 'morning star' and 'little angle' was understandable. However, loving a stranger was a phenomenon that neither she nor her husband had ever encountered.

As Mary's dad regarded the unusual scene, a work of grace gradually began to unfurl in his soul. Slowly but surely, through the picture of unconditional love that was played out in his living room, Mr McMillan began to comprehend the nature of the divine heart. His daughter's total acceptance of a foreign and broken child assaulted and captured the ramparts of his heart. If Mary Stevenson could cherish a foreigner, regardless of her condition, surely God would accept an unworthy sinner like him. With an enormous sense of inadequacy and unworthiness, Mary's father took his place before God and accepted Christ as his Saviour. Without a word, or even her knowledge, Naomi's life had won a soul for the Lord.

After a steady diet of 'Ulster Frys' not to mention lots of Belfast's traditional though greasy 'fish suppers' Billy was ready and fit for surgery. Doctor Johnston proved an adept and skilful surgeon and within a matter of weeks, the patient was on the mend and rearing to get back to work. However, much to Billy's surprise, the invasive and radical treatment left a legacy of fatigue that he hadn't anticipated. But, before he realised what was happening, Olga Leckie, wife of his old friend, James Leckie's nephew, Sandy, arrived to take him straight from his hospital sick bed to her father's Windsor Hotel situated in the pretty seaside town of Portrush. Ensconced in a luxury suite on the top floor of the building, Billy spent the next two weeks convalescing and gathering his strength. While the grateful patient enjoyed the good food and excellent nursing care, neither he nor Mary appreciated Olga's attempt to give him a haircut. By the time she had finished hacking and shearing, Billy could have won a starring role in a horror movie!

As the months passed and his health improved, the Belfast missionary found, that instead of South Korea, he was bound for the chilly coasts of Scotland. Mary accompanied him for several of the seminars and meetings, but their children's welfare, not to mention her increasing difficulties with health, confined her to home. On one occasion, as winter approached and the weather continued to worsen, Billy began to think that he too would be happier beside the comforting warmth of his mother's hearth. However, as the only speaker engaged for a conference in Inverness, Billy felt he had little choice but to do his best to turn up for the event. When a thick blanket of ice and snow froze all the nation's runways, clogging the arterial network of major airports, it seemed that he would have to cancel his appointment. Realising what an enormous upheaval such disappointment would cause to organisers as well as individuals, Billy decided to contact a friend that owned a small private aircraft and who might be willing to lend it for the trip. Within a couple of hours, he had successfully secured the use of the plane as well as the services of its pilot.

Once the tentative permission from Belfast's Met Office had been agreed, the little group was ready for take-off. However, it appeared that the pilot was locked in a dispute regarding the landing venue at Inverness. As the experts wrangled over the difficulties of bringing the aircraft down in such foul conditions, Billy grew more and more frustrated. Finally in a bid to get airborne, he suggested they implement the

Christian remedy. All they had to do was concentrate on getting off the ground and let God worry about the details of getting them down again!   Over an hour later, as they soared miles above the icy clouds, believing they were just moments from their Scottish destination, the radio crackled into life. Unable to see any familiar landmarks, the pilot of the lightweight aircraft requested permission to land at their designated venue. With shock and dismay, the crew learned that they had strayed miles off course and were totally lost. For Billy, the only difference between his experiences in Seoul and the current situation was that, instead of walking by faith, he was now flying by it! They may not be able to see the way ahead but God did. With nothing but a voice disjointed by radio static, they were guided back on course to the correct airfield where they landed blindly but safely. The Scottish conference went ahead and was richly blessed.

While prayer was a prominent feature in all of Billy's gospel rallies and conferences, a subsequent trip to Ayrshire in Scotland had him begging for Mary's life. During an annual seminar, the Irishman happened to notice that his wife was taking an unusually long time in the ladies rest room. Eventually, he sent one of the women to see what was keeping her. Agitated and upset the woman emerged with the news that Mary had collapsed and was in urgent need of medical attention. Thankfully, a doctor was among the Christian audience and he immediately called for an ambulance. Within an hour Mary was admitted to the intensive care department of the local hospital where she was diagnosed to be suffering from a serious heart complaint. Taking Billy and the children back to his home, the young doctor and his wife did their best to comfort the distraught husband. But when an emergency call insisted they return immediately to the high dependency unit, the medical man confessed that Mary's condition was deteriorating rapidly. Looking at his young family, Billy's heart broke. Isabelle and William needed their mother while Naomi, vulnerable and helpless, relied on her for everything. Regardless of the children's needs, how could he survive without the woman he loved? Heedless of everything save his family's desperation, the despondent husband and father fell on his knees and pleaded with God to spare Mary's life. By the time they had raced through the darkened streets and entered the hospital, Billy knew that his prayers had been answered. His wife, although ill, was no longer on the critical list. With tears of joy, Billy grasped her hand and thanked God for yet another instance of His mercy and grace.

Billy and Mary's furlough in Belfast lasted almost a year. It was dominated by broken health and painful operations but it wasn't only husband and wife who experienced a few medical dramas. Little Naomi, also underwent the traumatic but essential intervention of the surgeon's knife. Unable to comprehend the necessity for her tiny bones to be broken, re-shaped and held together by a plaster cast that reached from her chin to her feet, the South Korean infant could only rely on the wisdom of her mother's choices and the comfort of her arms.

Chapter 17
CHANGES AHEAD

THE LAST thing Mary Stevenson felt like was a five thousand mile journey back to South Korea. Her reluctance had nothing to do with the prospect of returning to life in Seoul. On the contrary she couldn't wait to see Chung Sook, Harabudji and their many other friends. Neither did fear of flying damper her enthusiasm. Undoubtedly, events of the last twelve months had left her emotionally drained. Within a short space of time, she had rocketed to the summit of joy at her dad's salvation before plummeting to the depths of sorrow at his death. However, Mary's inability to summon either interest or passion for the three long and tiring flights was based on physical weakness and exhaustion. Apart from a diagnosis of chronic heart problems, recurrent bouts of dizziness were once again taking their toll. Finally, just a couple of weeks prior to their departure, the mother of three was admitted to Belfast's Samaritan Hospital where she underwent an emergency hysterectomy. Nevertheless, bags had been packed, flights reserved and against medical advice, Mary decided to ignore her problems and continue with their plans.

During their absence, the city of Seoul had made rapid economic progress. The construction of the Sejong Centre for performing arts may have taken four years but in 1978, the largest complex in the capital finally opened its doors to the public. With an interior floor space of just over five hundred thousand square feet, the huge building was created to pay homage to the country's artistic heritage. But cultural celebrations were not confined to South Korea. The same year the Republic of China lifted its ban on the works of Aristotle, William Shakespeare and Charles Dickens. Yet, while the fleeting nature of classical literature gained acceptance, the Word of God, with the power to change lives and save souls for eternity, remained forbidden and ignored.

The family's return to South Korea was greeted with an enthusiastic welcome. Mary, forgetting the affects of jet lag, rushed to embrace Chung Sook, eager to catch up with the latest news. With heavily accented English that bore a strong resemblance to Mary's Ulster brogue, the girl who had come to them as lonely teenager, revealed that she was about to be married. The occasion, while a cause for happy celebrations, also provided Billy with a unique opportunity to take the gospel to another level of society. As stenographer to the South Korean government, Chung Sook's new husband arranged for Billy to speak at the important and influential centre of the country's administration. The parliamentary audience may have contrasted greatly with those Billy addressed at Seoul's army bases, leprosy colony and prisons, nevertheless, while the listeners may have changed, the message remained the same.

Initially there was no indication that, as a family, their time in South Korea was drawing to a close. The weekly Bible studies and gospel meetings that began in the home of local Christian man, Park Joon Young and continued in the Stevenson's living room, gained in both numbers and strength. Even Billy's illness was not permitted to interrupt the Lord's work. During his furlough in Ireland, husband and wife team, John and Rene Anderson took over Billy's adult Bible class, inviting students to meet at their house. Before long, the demand for a larger meeting place resulted in the establishment of Shilim Dong, a much welcomed gospel hall. Other hard working individuals, among them, Eddie James and Doug Neiswender played a major role in ensuring that similar halls were created in the surrounding areas. Yet Mary's unrelenting heath problems combined with the increasing needs of Naomi's medical care became a predominant feature of Billy's prayers. He knew that as his adopted daughter grew, she would require even more specialised attention. Equally he understood that without finance they would not be able to meet the challenge. With a great sense of his human inadequacy and helplessness, Billy asked God to provide the solution.

The arrival of an American missionary at the Stevenson's home did not immediately appear to be the divine answer! Welcoming their distressed visitor, neither Billy nor Mary had any idea that he would become a stepping stone toward a new life. Quietly they listened as the troubled man unfolded his tale of woe. Years earlier, he had come to Seoul as a young soldier and fallen in love with a pretty local girl. Within a few months the couple had married and returned to live in the States where, as Christians they enjoyed the warmth of an assembly fellowship. But memories of the great need amongst the South Korean people, combined with a passion to serve the Lord, had evoked a desire to work in the mission field.

Without waiting for a definite sense of divine guidance, he and his family had arrived; ill-equipped spiritually as well as emotionally to begin their evangelistic service among the city's lost and needy. It didn't take long to discover that the reality of a poverty stricken lifestyle did not compare with his idealistic dreams. Disillusioned and depressed, he turned to Billy for help. With gentle diplomacy, the Shankill Road man explained the need for God's seal of approval on every undertaking. Only the certainty of His will could lend fortitude and strength for the difficulties of the most arduous journeys. With great tenderness he advised the confused man to take his family and go home to America where, with mediation and prayer, he would find God's purpose for his life. Over the coming weeks, Billy's new friend set about returning to his home fellowship while his Korean wife stayed behind to deal with the formalities of moving house. Concerned at the thought of her travelling alone, her husband asked if Billy, along with another brother, would accompany her on the journey. The event was to herald a new chapter in the life of the whole Stevenson family.

Billy's arrival in Illinois brought immediate blessings. It also proved a watershed for his family as well as his individual service. Yet, at the time, the Irishman had no inkling that his life would changed irrevocably. Leaving the hospitality of his acquaintances, Billy travelled to meet with another missionary friend based in Chicago. During the visit, he was invited to have lunch with Mr Jim Starr, president of what was then know as the 'Interest Ministries' publication and, naturally, the conversation turned to the Stevenson family's experience of life in the Korean mission field.

Little by little Billy told the interested businessman of the great work that was taking place in the East. He explained about the success of their home Bible study and Sunday school classes, the support received both from the local community and other missionaries. His enthusiasm for the 'Seekers Hour' gospel radio broadcast was evident as was his delight at the public's response. With numerous stories of grace, Billy revealed their life among the people they had come to love. Yet, regardless of the many examples of divine providence, there was no account more touching than the tender description of Naomi's adoption. Despite the softly spoken tones, Billy's expression was animated by the sheer delight of parental love. He and Mary had been blessed with two healthy children whom they cherished. Yet, in the natural course of events, Isabelle and William would one day take their place in adult society. They would have the opportunity to marry, raise children of their own and lead an independent life. But, Naomi, locked in a world of helpless innocence would always rely on the mercy of others. Her vulnerable and broken condition demanded the kind of service that could only be a labour of love. From the moment they agreed to take her into their home, Billy and Mary accepted the responsibility and the blessing of such a commitment.

As the conversation continued long into the afternoon, the doors of Billy's heart opened and his pent up emotions poured out. Articulately he described, not only his wife's battle against the disorientating effects of vertigo and fatigue, but their children's brave attempts to cope with the complexities of their family situation. Moved by the candid revelations, Jim Starr offered, what Billy suddenly realised, was a miraculous answer to prayer!

Incredulously, Billy listened as he extended an invitation for Mary and the children to be treated, free of charge, at one of Chicago's Stewart Foundation clinics that specialised in the care of missionaries and their families. Weak with relief but bubbling over with gratitude, he thanked his new friend for such an amazing act of generosity and kindness. Their meeting at an end, the men shook hands and they parted company. Mr Starr, no doubt continued with the business of the day unaware of the train of events he had set in motion. Meanwhile, the only priority on Billy's list was to find a phone and tell his wife how God had once again exceeded all their expectations!

In a tumult of emotion, Mary listened as her husband re-capped the day's events. Eager to convey the full import of what Mr Starr was offering before the transatlantic connection failed, he omitted much of the finer details. When Mary finally replaced the receiver, she looked around the room and knew her life had changed direction. She had no idea what lay ahead but, just as she had followed her husband to Seoul, she would now join him in America. Their path had taken a sudden and unexpected twist, yet the knowledge that God was in control, lent a sense of peace. Hurriedly she set about the now familiar preparations for departure. By the time she had kissed Chung Sook goodbye, hoisted Naomi onto her hip and shepherded Isabelle and William toward the waiting plane, Mary already felt the first tremors of excitement.

several months of traction combined with numerous sessions of physiotherapy, doctors were unable to find a remedy and had no option but to discharge Mary, leaving her to seek an alternative solution. Nevertheless, any doubt that their journey to America had been in vain was soon swept away. Instead of a medical environment, Mary found the answer to her spinning world in the unlikely setting of a Sunday morning service when, one of the sisters, a chiropractor's wife, suggested that her husband may be able to help. At first, both Mary and Billy responded with a smile of polite scepticism. They had explored every possible avenue of medical expertise, not only in America but in Belfast, Scotland and Korea. From a diet of seaweed soup to hour upon hour of immobilised and stretched muscles, Mary had tried every conceivable remedy yet nothing had worked. Undaunted the chiropractor's wife persisted until, in an attempt to indulge her kindness, Mary agreed to a prescribed course of therapy.

Initially, the repetitive and sometimes painful, massage appeared to achieve little but gradually, Mary began to notice her world settling to a more static position. Slowly, the orbital sensation ceased and the ecstatic woman realised the treatment had worked! Apparently, her problem began several years earlier when, walking along the streets of Seoul, she had been on the head hit by a heavy sign hanging over a shop doorway. The impact had forced her spine to compact, pressing on nerves that affected her balance. With obvious relief, Mary was once again able to hold her head high.

Within a few months, it appeared that life in America was strewn with every imaginable blessing. Mary's health was better than it had ever been, the children had settled well and best of all, Billy had the privilege of, not only returning to South Korea as a guest speaker but touring the states of America with God's message of salvation. As they took their places among the fellowship at Warrenville Bible Chapel, and looked at the faces of God's people who had welcomed them with such warmth, their hearts soared with praise. From the moment of their arrival in Chicago, many wonderful people had entered their life and with incredible displays of kindness had tended to the family's every spiritual, medical and even financial need. Their friends' obvious love for Naomi as they fussed and hugged her affectionately was an added joy. Neither were the tender displays of consideration and compassion confined to their Christian fellowship. No matter where she went, Naomi added a sparkle of happiness that brightened everyone's day. Whether in the small local stores or big city malls, her huge grin of delight at life's simplest pleasure was enough to elicit a friendly smile from many passers-by. However, as Mary and Billy had discovered, their adopted daughter often evoked more than an affable acknowledgement. Husband and wife had learned to recognise when the casual flicker of interest in Naomi's history turned to more profound thoughts of divine love. Their Korean daughter's life may have begun as a portrait of rejection and weakness but it had rapidly proved a powerful illustration of grace. Billy had preached many sermons but there was none so eloquent as that of Naomi's life.

In those early days as they basked in the warm rays of friendship and plenty, the hardships of South Korea seemed a long way away. Perhaps as she looked at her children's healthy complexion and the kitchen cupboards filled with food, Mary breathed a word of thanks for the new season in her life. Little did she know that, while America offered rest for her soul, it also held the severest trial of her faith. Perhaps the first indication that the still waters were about to be replaced by an arduous mountain climb began with what appeared to be a bout of indigestion. When a friend who happened to be a specialist in the problems associated with eyes, ears, nose and throat, invited Billy to speak at a school in India, Billy readily accepted. Never confident of his technique or delivery, the Shankill Road man had learned long ago to ignore his own limitations and simply preach the Word of God. Every chance to tell others about God's amazing salvation was an opportunity not to be missed. Nevertheless, he found the niggling sensation of discomfort in his chest difficult to ignore. But, a couple of antacid tables and a few painkillers later, he boarded the plane and headed for India and the Bethseda School at Miraj; six hours journey south of Bombay.

Several hours later, just as he was about to address the Indian students, Billy realised that the crushing pain in his chest had nothing to do with poor digestion. Thankfully, his medical friend carried something other than ear syringes in his first aid kit. Placing the tiny nitro-glycerine pill under his tongue, Billy felt an immediate relief that enabled him to continue with his message. In fact, the medication worked so well that, over the next few days he was able to take the gospel to the student nurses and doctors working during the late night shift in the surrounding hospitals. In the early morning, as he breakfasted on grapes from the local vines, the gripping pains had become a distant memory. However, although the symptoms had faded, Billy's heart condition remained and by the time he returned to Chicago, it was obvious he needed to visit his doctor. Yet, the news that Mary's brother was seriously ill, followed by the discovery that a close family member had been diagnosed with cancer and Billy's problems suddenly dropped down the list of priorities. In the normal course of events, the tragic circumstances would have seemed a heavy load. But combined with the fatigue of constant long distance travelling, ailing health and the rapidly increasing dependency of Naomi, they added an unbearable strain.

Desperate to visit her brother in Ireland before he died, Mary knew they needed to find professional care for Naomi. Their older children, both busy with their own lives had sufficient problems with neither resources nor ability for their adopted sister's needs. Realising that the young girl would find separation a distressing and confusing experience, she and Billy did their best to select a small but efficient nursing facility near their home. Clutching her doll, Naomi smiled and waved goodbye to the only parents she had ever known. Mary and Billy drew comfort from the fact they would be gone little more than a few days and hoped they would pass quickly.

As with all periods of grief and sorrow, time spent comforting her family flew rapidly by. Yet the hours until she could be re-united with Naomi merely dragged. Within a few of days, Mary and Billy were back in America, rushing toward the care unit, eager to take their daughter home.   However, there were no smiles or whoops of delight to welcome their return. Naomi was distraught, frightened, and tearful. The doll she had once cradled and stroked for comfort was tossed aside with angry frustration. Locked in a world of silence, she could neither vent her feelings nor explain the events that triggered them. Understandably, alarmed, the couple tried to discover the reason for such uncharacteristic behaviour. Medical opinion determined that Naomi had suffered some form of physical and emotional trauma but despite all endeavours and investigations, they met only a wall of silence. Only another parent can experience the raw emotions at the knowledge their child has suffered abuse and are helpless to redress the situation. With time, patience and a lot of perseverance, Naomi's smile slowly returned. Whatever horror had caused her trauma was pushed to the recesses of her memory as she once again giggled and played with her new doll. But, Mary and Billy endured many nights of tortured anguish as the dreadful images of what might have happened crowded their minds. Overloaded with stress and torn by his inability to protect Naomi, Billy was about to embark on a once familiar and devastating course.

Chapter 19
BIRD WITH A BROKEN WING
෯

JUST A year into the Millennium and Northern Ireland's reputation as a nation of fighters was once again making the headlines. But on this occasion, the people involved, ensured that any punches were conducted with self control and restraint. Held in Belfast's Odyssey Arena, the World Amateur Boxing Championships attracted around four hundred boxers from a record sixty seven countries and, with six reigning world champions among the participants, the event was an enormous success. Thousands of miles from the convivial atmosphere of Belfast, India was mourning the loss of twenty thousand people after an earthquake measuring 7.9 on the Richter Scale brought chaos and destruction in its wake. Yet, regardless of individual celebrations or national catastrophes, there was only one event that indelibly branded society's collective memory. A terrorist attack on New York's World Trade Centre during the morning of 11th September 2001, removed the famous Twin Towers from the city's landscape and tore thousands of loved ones from their families. The cost in monetary terms was astronomical but the price of human suffering was inestimable.

Billy was driving along the freeway on a return journey from Arkansas to their new home in Florida, when a friend rang Mary's mobile to tell them the horrific news. Stunned, by the magnitude of the event, the couple drove along in silence, each immersed in their own thoughts. The force of evil that had precipitated such an act of cruelty and carnage was beyond their comprehension. At the sound of Naomi, strapped safely in the back seat of the car, playing with her doll and blissfully unaware of man's inhumanity to man, Mary and Billy prayed for the bereaved and offered thanks for their blessings. Later the same day, Billy was in the middle of his own medical drama. The pain and discomfort he had experienced in India came back with a vengeance. Instead of returning home for a relaxing evening, the reluctant patient was admitted to hospital where he underwent an operation to help unblock an artery in his heart. The widely used procedure that involves inserting a wire metal mesh tube known as a 'Stent' into the affected area, is usually highly successful but, in Billy's case, the remedy failed and his condition became a matter of urgency. There was no alternative; the Irish man was facing a major operation.

Whatever side affects Billy anticipated from the by-pass surgery, he was not prepared for the bleak cloud of depression that sapped every ounce of emotional strength. Desperately he tried to hide his feelings, hoping that as time passed, they would fade and disappear. But the suffocating blackness would not relinquish its hold. Instead it spread and infiltrated each realm of his life including his ability to pray. Drowning in the awful sea of apathy, he clung to his faith. However, he knew that his grip was weakening and he would soon be drifting aimlessly and lost. In his fragile emotional state, even the minor obstacles of life seemed as impossible hurdles. But further complications with health pushed him over the edge. A diagnosis of prostrate cancer instigated yet more rounds of hospital visits, unpleasant treatments and yet another infusion of depression. When prescriptions for sedatives, painkillers and antidepressants failed to dispel the gloom, Billy finally turned to an old and deceptively reliable form of anaesthetic.

Initially, the alcoholic remedy remained a hidden solace to be applied in the hours of darkness when symptoms were most acute. But gradually, as the need increased Billy no longer cared that his failure, both as a Christian and as a provider for his family, was evident. His only desire was the numbing effects that alcohol offered. For Mary, the discovery that her husband was drinking again, added an indefinable burden. Confused and frightened by the unforeseen turn of events, she turned to God for comfort and guidance. Their life in South Korea had been hard. Many times they had gone without food and bare essentials but never had she had encountered such a flaw in Billy's faith. Memories of a life where drink cast its unpredictable and disruptive influence came flooding back. She could not comprehend how her husband, as a Christian man, would turn in such a direction. As the weeks progressed, Mary Stevenson had never spent so much time on her knees.

Unheeding and, to the point of uncaring, Billy rocketed further out of control. Eventually, fuelled by drink he left the house and stumbled toward a place where he could rest in the arms of oblivion. That night, drunk and helpless, he sank to his knees on what appeared a grassy and pleasant knoll. Laying his head on the soft sweet ground, Billy succumbed to the seduction of sleep. Next morning, hung over and thirsty he woke to an unrelenting headache and the knowledge that he had been sharing his bed with alligators and snakes! In his confused and inebriated state, Billy had wandered into one of Florida's many swamps and slept amongst some of the world's most dangerous creatures. Yet, God had preserved him and not a single finger or toe had been nibbled. Leaving the reptilian inhabitants to their own devices, he made his way toward an urban jungle, infested with a different but equally hazardous species.

Walking along the street, Billy's mind was in a turmoil of despair and initially did not notice the young men who circled and surrounded him. As they closed in on their prey and demanded he part with his wedding ring, Billy's old temper flared. Never, in all the time since he had confessed Christ as Saviour had he allowed himself to become embroiled in the demeaning and dishonourable situation of a brawl. Of course, there had been an occasional moment when racial remarks concerning Naomi had provided temptation. Yet, apart from throwing an apple pie in true slapstick style due to frustrated annoyance, he had never punched anyone. Suddenly, the intensity of his angry feelings surprised and frightened him. Ignoring the outcome of certain injury he challenged his opponents to remove the object of their desire with force.

Throughout his life, God had intervened at moments of deepest despair. At every need He had provided an instrument of grace. James Leckie had been the chosen vessel in the alleyways of Belfast while Eddie James, Wesley Barr and many others had proved a blessing in South Korea. Jim Starr had constructed the bridge that led them to America. Sophus Bolt and his wife had undertaken the physical and financial needs with the provision of their first home in Chicago. Even mundane requirements like plumbing had been met through their friendship with Maurice Martin. Billy and Mary knew the enormous debt of gratitude they owed God's people but equally they understood their inability to repay. Yet, they rested in the certainty that every act of kindness would, one day receive its reward.

Undoubtedly, Mary and Billy had encountered many Good Samaritans throughout their journey. But the one who came to stop a fight and bring Billy home was perhaps the most blessed of all. Dressed in his police uniform, the man of God arrived at the scene and, after scattering the thugs, listened to Billy's incredible story. As the man before him poured out his history in Ireland, his encounter with God and his service in South Korea, tears welled in the officer's eyes at his subsequent failure in America. With non judgemental compassion he explained how Billy's wife and friends had spent the night searching his whereabouts, eager for his safe return. Gently, the young policeman placed Billy in the back of his car and drove him home. There were no words of condemnation, only a promise that, as no crime had been committed; there would be no further mention of the incident.

While his wife offered support and prayer, it was Billy's daughter who provided understanding. At one time, her dad had played the role of hero but Isabelle knew that heroes are merely the characters of fairy tales and a little girl's view of her father. Maturity and life had shown her that man does not belong on a pedestal. Even a cursory knowledge of scripture teaches that the most faithful of God's men had their weaknesses and failures. Life may have orchestrated a series of trials that her dad could not surmount but it didn't detract from his service or faith. With gentle words, Isabelle reassured and reminded her dad that God had not forgotten him. Encouraged, Billy took his place before the Throne of Grace and begged for mercy. Like many before him, he too received the immeasurable value of divine pardon. Contrite and ashamed, he also sought Mary's forgiveness. The years had neither dulled nor detracted from his wife's love and with without a moment's hesitation, Billy was fully restored in his wife's estimation.

No doubt Billy could have let the matter rest but, after so many selfless acts of kindness, he felt that his assembly fellowship had the right to know about his failure. Calling a meeting he determined to reveal his recent exploits but by the time the designated appointment arrived he was overcome with apprehension. Perhaps, after listening to the catalogue of shame, his Christian friends may decide to abandon him. Finally, confronted by the friendly but expectant faces, Billy began to tell a story about a bird who suffered a broken wing. As the tale progressed, his audience heard how a little bird once soared above the earth with strength and purpose. Yet, when it encountered the hard surface of an unexpected obstacle, it had plummeted useless to the ground. Regardless, of how much, the creature wanted to fly its fragile condition rendered it useless but a gentle and compassionate person found the bird and took it home. With perseverance, kindness and care, the wing gradually mended until one day, the gentle benefactor opened the window and the grateful bird flew away. Admitting that he too had suffered a broken wing, Billy used the analogy to illustrate his life. After a moment's stunned silence, the sound of chairs scraping against the floor's surface revealed the meeting was over but it was each individual embrace of love that told Billy he had been forgiven. Regardless of what he had received in the past, it was the gift of brotherly compassion that was most precious of all.

Epilogue
FLYING HIGH

A FEW years after his reminder that wings are fragile and prone to fracture, Billy Stevenson is once again airborne. Despite the interruption of life's chaos and distractions, his service has not been terminated. Aware of the immense grace that has been bestowed upon him, his preaching has adopted a new dimension of humility and power. The physical limitations of bodily health may occasionally impose a few restrictions but Billy continues to travel the world, telling others of God's love and salvation. His frequent trips to South Korea bring immense satisfaction that, despite everything, the work continues to grow. In India he witnesses to the young students at Bethseda School while, in Northern Ireland and throughout America, his ministry is received with warm appreciation.

In moments of pensive reflection, Billy recalls their time in the poverty stricken streets of Seoul as among the happiest in his life. Total dependence upon God, although sometimes difficult, is always an exhilarating and beneficial experience. As with all who have tripped and stumbled, Billy Stevenson has been left with an acute sense of his own frailty but equally he has experienced the profound depths of divine love. Both he and Mary are eternally grateful for the care and prayers of those in the assembly fellowship at Warrenville Bible Chapel in Chicago and their present place of worship, Carolwood Bible Chapel in Tampa, Florida. These wonderful people of God who have shown the Stevenson family the true character of Christian love. Constraints of time and space prevent mention of the many individuals who have supported and nurtured Mary and Billy through some of the most difficult times. Yet, the couple delights in the knowledge that every name and act of kindness is recorded in Heaven.

Mary, now approaching her seventy-seventh birthday, remains dedicated to the care of her South Korean daughter. Even in her autumnal years, there is no sense of heavy responsibility, let alone burden. Aided by caring professionals like Fannie whose recent salvation has added a note of joy to the household, Mary delights in what she views as her labour of love. Pragmatism and humour may be her dominant characteristics but it is impossible to mistake the underlying core of faith.

William and Isabelle, Mary's 'Morning Star' and 'Little Angel,' have, as predicted, been blessed with independence and success. As adults, brother and sister have maintained their individual faith and gone on to serve the Lord in their respective fields. Now in her thirties, Naomi has recently discovered the thrill of modern technology. The acquisition of a doll that addresses her as 'mama' plus the high tech manoeuvres of her new wheel chair are a constant source of excitement and pleasure.

There is no doubt that Billy and Mary's life has been dedicated to the love of Naomi but ultimately, such a service can only be to the glory of God.